Home Is Where
An Anthology of African American Poetry
from the Carolinas

For
Cindy and John
On Poetry
and
Friendship,
Lenard D. Moore
June 12, 2012

Thank you
Cindy. 6/12/12
Ayoba Joy

Jaki Shelton Green
in Peace!

Home Is Where

An Anthology of African American Poetry
from the Carolinas

edited by Kwame Dawes

Hub City Press
Spartanburg, SC

First printing, November 2011

Book design: Mark Pointer
Cover art: Alvin Staley

Home is where : an anthology of African American poetry from the Carolinas / [compiled by] Kwame Dawes.
p. cm.
ISBN 978-1-891885-80-8 (pbk.)
1. American poetry--African American authors. 2. American poetry--21st century. 3. African Americans--Poetry. 4.
North Carolina--Poetry. 5. South Carolina--Poetry. 6. Southern states--Poetry. I. Dawes, Kwame Senu Neville, 1962- II.
Title: African American poetry from the Carolinas.
PS591.N4H56 2011
811'.540808960730756--dc22
2011008144

186 West Main Street
Spartanburg SC 29306
864-577-9349 www.hubcity.org

For
Lorna
Sena, Kekeli and Akua

For
Gwyneth, Kojo, Aba, Adjoa, and Kojovi

For
Mama the Great
Remembering Neville

But when my bleeding feet came to the end,

And I was bound and scourged by cruel fate;

Alas, I cried, pray let me start again.

It was too late.

"Experience" by James E. McGirt (North Carolina, 1874-1930)

Home is Where

INTRODUCTION
Home Is Where
By Kwame Dawes

This anthology seeks to celebrate the strength that exists in the work of African American poets in the Carolinas region. Many of them are scattered all around the country now, and these poets show themselves to have a great deal in common by being poets who have roots in this region. At the same time, many of the poets collected here have, like me, adopted the Carolinas as home, as places of cultural and imaginative definition.

Here, then, is a gathering of poets that is exciting. I have not sought to select poems that are "about" the South or about the Carolinas, especially. Instead, I called for poems and then selected the poems that I believed were the strongest, most evocative and consistent with the evolving spirit of the anthology. I have been as interested in showing range (of style, theme, form, and language) as I have in simply choosing poems I like. The latter criteria is decidedly biased, but I do not apologize for this as I believe that my tastes are not so limiting to make the collection monochromatic, plain, or predictable, and are not so eclectic as to deprive the work of a unity of artistic taste that I believe is necessary in any good book, in any solid anthology.

Instead, what I believe we have collected here is, first and foremost, a wonderful collection of poems by poets who range from the fully accomplished to those who are making their first outing.

This, then, is a proud collection—a collection that the region should be proud of. I know, for certain, that people will be surprised to see some names in this anthology, poets they might have known of, but poets they had no idea were from either of our states.

The truth is that only those who do not come from this region routinely mistake the two states. In my experience, the tendency for people outside of the region is to default by lumping both states into North Carolina. The differences between the two states are numerous and are not isolated simply to football and barbecue. Our histories are quite different, and so are our demographics. However, there is much that connects these two states.

The things that unify us are obvious: the shared name, the long history of slavery, the tradition of resistance to slavery and the attendant years of Jim Crow, the strong sense of place and commitment to the land, the burden of stigma associated with being from the "Deep South" or the "Bible Belt," the extended history of faith founded heavily in Christian traditions, and a long list of names of people who left, became great, and constantly surprised the world with the discovery that they were born and raised in one of these states.

Regional anthologies allow us to give attention to poets who might be excluded from national anthologies, not because of the quality of the work, but because of the limitations of the idea of nation that one cannot avoid. What is most encouraging to me with this anthology is that after the call for poems was sent out to a list of over one hundred poets, I got responses from virtually all the established black poets in and from the region, as well as a rich pool of poems from less established but equally interesting poets who are willing to regard either North or South Carolina as home. From this pool, I was able to make selections that I believe represent an engaging picture of where contemporary poetry is in our states, and, by extension, in the country.

I became a citizen of the United States of America about three years ago, some sixteen years after arriving in South Carolina to teach. The curious thing about becoming a U.S. citizen was that it arrived long after I had embraced my position as a South Carolinian. One of the most important factors in shaping my affinity to this state and this region has been the process of working through my position as a black person among black people living in this country. The Gullah culture, the long history of slavery and segregation, and the genius of survival through language, art, faith, and community are all things that have drawn me into this community.

As a Pan Africanist, and a child of the African Diaspora, I have long found affinity and belonging in the recognition of the grander scheme of migration, dislocation, and survival that is the story of people of the African Diaspora. This truth has been no less relevant here in the Carolinas. More than anything else, the poems in this collection are about the troubling idea of "home. It is "home" that drives the construction of the collection, and based on a reading of the work, it is the idea of home that has engaged so many of our poets.

Evie Shockley's poem, "home is where," therefore provided the

Home is Where

perfect title for this collection. What follows the phrase "home is where" may be a question mark, an ellipsis, or a series of clichés, phrases, musings, and contemplations that can ultimately emerge as poems. The most obvious of those clichés, "home is where the heart is," turns out to be the defining complexity of the poems in this collection even when some of the poets write about exile from a home that has not always been very welcoming to them.

There is fierce love, belonging, and loyalty for the Carolinas in these poems, and yet, at the same time, the poems express what is always true about home—that it is a place that both embraces and rejects us; a place that we adore and resent; a place we understand deeply and   remain perplexed by. In these poems, these wonderful contradictions are revealed in beautiful language, deft craft, splendid improvisations and experimentation, and thematic range.

Above everything else, this is a collection of fine poetry and for any reader, the quality of the work and its range may come as a pleasant surprise—a beautiful, varied, tantalizing, and fresh body of work. I am deeply pleased with the power of the work collected here, and it is my hope that others will share in my view that what we experience as we read this collection is a beautiful exposure to the best of American poetry today.

Kwame Dawes
Columbia, SC, August 2011

at last

...for Etta James

the hefty, yellow skinned woman
bellowed, her raspy voice scratchin'
the dusky, underbelly of the blues.
a bourbon thrown back, no one
could tell her about love. and everyone
who heard her
knew she had been scarred,
really bruised deep down inside
that last time she settled for a honeymoon.

you smiled... she remembered
the jaunty days when their love was green and wild
with abandon. she trusted her heart
that where ever she ended up, she was fully capable
of landing on her feet. sure,
even though she was really a city girl
and used to the rough and tumble,
she rather liked the idea of being *wrapped in clover,*
of being enclosed, protected for once —

in her hoped-for world, she would chant, *my love has come along*
just like the yellow woman belting
out her songs, the grand conjunction of pain and bruised memory
encircled like a knotted sleeve.

she hoped the *lonely days were over,* but like the woman
in the *song* said, she needed
a thrill to press her cheek to or at least,
a spell cast
in heaven, something, at any rate
to bring her luck in love.

Italics indicates lyrics from the song, "At Last" as sung by Etta James.

Home is Where

stepping

...Cincinnati, Ohio, 1961

when you saw him steppin' sideways to a gal,
he was drunker than a skunk.

oh you can't say that...
it's such a cliché—

cliché or not, he was toasted,
a down in the gutter drunk
soggy and swaying near the corner.
the first day i saw him.
...just didn't understand that strange posture, the curved human
where a man should have stood.

when i was nine, he first passed
walking tall, in his grand sky boots
texas style, leaning heavily in those rough-hewn heels,
a ten gallon cocked to the side...
slow and measured, he lifted each boot
as if expecting the sidewalk to meet his steps half way.
hours down, walking back up from the bar,
he stepped more slowly

as if searching for cotton to pad his strides.

and did i say how red his eyes were,
how burned and diffused or how they must have mirrored
the depth of pain he could hardly now name—

did he want his manhood back,
the space to expand into his own dimension of strength
instead of the roped off areas
a black was expected to inhabit—

but he couldn't get past that confinement

unless he drank his way through.
even after empting the bottle, consuming
past what should have been his normal limits...

drinking seemed preferable to real breath—

hardest to swallow
was the consumption past one's own limit,
as if being forced to hold one's head
below water
long after one needed breath...

so watt is possible for a black man
especially when the vision of himself has been truncated,
pressed down and left behind in the dregs of an upturned bottle—

JAZZ MAN

Jazz Man,
Play me a lullaby.
Create the tune
that flows through my veins
and escapes in my smile.

Bring in the saxophone
if I close my eyes.
I won't get upset.
I'll just fall more in love
with that high pitched perfection.

Bring in the drums
if my head gets heavy.
I won't mind.
Maybe it will scare away
whatever goes bump in the night.

Bring in the clarinet
if my heart gets weak.
I won't be afraid.
It will remind me
of my people.

Cause Mr. Jazz Man you're no Coltrane, but you will do.

THEY SAY THE MOONFLOWER BLOOMS AT NIGHT

the dreamer wears a crown on his heart.
he's been planting flowers in her garden,
watering them with jewels
and reaching for silver sunlight
in the morning air.

even when his voice is dry,
he floods her door with poems
and takes them, one by one,
drawing lines in the sand.

the dreamer plucks lilies from silence
and lavender from the ether,
hoping that love will blossom.
what lies beneath the root is truth,

watered down to the soul.

WITH LUNA

tonight, the moon is a woman
and she is our escape.
her silver shadow hangs thick
over a horizon of sleepy stars
and her eyes make bold advances
toward the sun.

you are her favorite daughter –
a lunar eclipse among stargazers,
unaffected by the sky's flirtation with dawn.

i am nothing more than earthshine –
orbiting into daydreams,
silently reflecting her light.

JUNE'S BLUES

There's a black bluesman with a dust-covered axe
For his daughter he worked overtime with bosses on his back
Daughter bore her father's features some folk called her copycat
Cause the daughter like her poppa took to choppin, took a wife
Yes. The daughter took to choppin, took a wife.

Took the black bluesman his mannish daughter for a son
Taught her how to push a mower just to churn them out some coins
Then one day while she was toilin 'gainst both circumstance and sun
Family name became her carriage, Poppa's work down here was done
Yes. The father's days of earthly work were done.

So the black bluesman chose to hasten to his throne
His body dressed for Galilee as the cancer honeycombed
Congregations speak of heaven but however kingdom come
Hope it don't got toil or bosses just a place for axe and moan.
Yes. A bluesman needs a heaven, host his moans.

SUB-GOLDSBORO GARAGE GALS

a woman's body is the universal shelter
                    —June Jordan

Propped in sleek recline,
chipped cinder loafs as amateur amazons
scan hooded vehicles for leaky lubricants,
a grimacing gran torino,
glued grounded by a gluttonous gasket,
greets a girlish sub-Goldsboro gang
who done graduated to grassy garage gals
since Granddaddy's gone

Buried beneath this weak wreckage,
women wet with winced whisky
wear wild weekends to weather workday weariness;
they rear a wedlocked litter
wrenching a rusty, worn oil filter
with a family of phallic-less, faultless fingers

Round where wheat lice weeds and winds
washpots wait on wood heaters to warm winter water
warning weary women who wear make-do wisdom
to wade every once in a while

STRINGING CIGARETTES

For Grandmamma Ruth

My grandmamma Ruth could string tobacco
leaf cigarettes
onto a tobacco cigarette stick faster than
any tie-down red head rag Negro
morning woman
under the sad sun
and the shed of a tired Monday
rundown cigarette tobacco barn.
On either side,
a tobacco hander would hand
to my grandmamma
Ruth a hand full of cigarette leaves
and she would
twist a tight string this way,
tie-back a tight loop
that way, while twisting another
string of cigarettes
the other way all in a one motion
hurried blue blur.
Lunch times were the best
of all the sun heavy hot
tobacco times I spent on tobacco farms,
in tobacco fields,
around the hard heavy presence of
tobacco
barns. I loved my lunch bucket
as much as I hated
the sound and smell of sun melted welfare cheese.
I learned how to shift gears
on a green John Deere tobacco green tractor
when I was eight and before
I turned ten years old, I knew

exactly when a ripe leaf
of tobacco was ripe to be picked
in a wrap around hand motion
from the bottom of a sand sag tobacco
tree. You may not know, but
tobacco field worms
have horns
and are full of nothing but green tobacco
juice. Tobacco snakes come in every color
but green. All the hard news Negro men
I knew cropped
tobacco
fields until they died,
the women and girls worked
side by side, close to the barn
before and after babies
and all the young cigarette boys
decided to stay
in the ruts and roads of life
with no definition,
stay in the arms of their own lunch buckets
or leave
fields after growing up quick
in the cigarette fire
of fields.
From a green world of nothing to find,
some went on to rice paddy fields
in Vietnam,
some went on to cities and towns
of light while
others simply disappeared in the cigarette
packs of tobacco
fields. I suppose, years later, when
the sad uneven dance was done,
sad newspapers
filled in the cracks, keeping the sad
winter from
seeping into the space between

the loops of
cigarettes
and telephone lines.
Grandmamma Ruth, I suppose, saw herself
young as the young
guitar playing strings
of tobacco road. All things,
again, alive and lit orange
by the orange colored
people's god, all things, again,
glowing orange
in the smoky blue haze of her last Carolina days.

Home is Where

TWO GEORGE WASHINGTONS

For Clarence Nixon

If I believed in the word *ironic,*
I would say it was ironic that when we
both were seventeen, my best friend was killed
when his car slid, then veered head first into
my George Washington Live tree oak, located
alone,
beside
highway number 17.
My tree was named by the Southern Daughters
of the American Revolution. And beneath her
shady
American Southern arms, I grew up to love
the way she hugged me close and tight
and away from the face
of the yellow sun, and even on days of torrential rain,
her 1776 umbrella let me not feel
a drop of the pain
of being five or maybe I was six,
hoping and praying
poverty was blind and
would not find me living
in a two room, back room shack
with my grandmother.
I loved the shady days of that tree
that decided to kill
Clarence one Southern summer night
some years after
we, my grandmamma and me, moved
from beneath her branches. Some years
are longer than other years.
1971 was longer than them all. Nubby,
we all called him
that because he was short and his voice,
soft and easy

as if he was afraid to say too much. Days
when we were stranded
between the stop signs of being stranded
in the sad summer months between
8th and 9th grade,
during daylight save no time in fields of
heat and blueberry
picking buckets, we spent all we earned
on new clothes
for our new white brick red school.
At summer's end,
Nubby and I hitched a long slow ride to town
and spent our pennies on green pants to match
our matchless gold puff sleeve shirts
to be worn the first day of high school. We
thought, I guess, it would make us look
cool. And we
were cool fools, two clowns in a town without
any slow Southern ice tea pity
from a white small town full of angry white people
angrily exchanging the exchanges
between envelopes and US postal stamps
stamping signs
of disapproval across the forehead of
the first day of
integration into a school that heretofore
disallowed
us, the niggers from niggerville,
to sit in the classroom
white desk chairs of higher white education. Nubby
was not smart,
he never learned much beyond acting up
and acting out in Mrs. Winter's history class. I guess
he just never realized that George Washington was white
as white notebook school boy notebook paper. And when
he told his mama that he did not cut down the cherry tree,
he was just telling a regular, everyday, ordinary white
notebook paper, white George Washington lie.

Home is Where

RAFTERS

The barn,
Gray and rotting where
The edges touch the wet earth,
Is filled to the rafters with things
We put away from one year to the next;
And out in the field,
Half hidden by the wild sprouts,
Is the old plow my father left
The last year he planted the crop
We deserted, never harvesting
What his sweat was meant for,
But left one by one for the factories,
Taking wives and husbands to make
Homes where the work was good
In the cities.
I think about the hot summer streets
When we sat on the cement stoops
Drinking beer on paydays
While our children grew farther
From our reach and one day
So far they could not hear
The sound of our voices calling
Through the night.
And I know now that what
We came for we didn't get,
And we have put away whatever
Plans we had.
I will leave the city
And try to pull the old plow
Out of the land,
Fix the bottom of the barn
With aged hands.

PEACH ORCHARD

Still I hear the flatbed truck
Rumbling down the road before sunup,
Waking me to the chatter of strong-shouldered men
With loose shirts smelling of Borax,
The high-pitched voices of girls waiting,
Crowding together for the pickup.
Mama will call us soon to get about
The yard work when it's light enough
To hitch out the cow in the high dewy grass
That stings the ankle sores
That never heal all summer.
The chickens are to be fed,
The hog slopped with the leftovers;
The old dog covered with ticks
Will wag his tail expecting a handout;
The kittens will cower underneath the barn.
And when the sun's too hot,
We young ones will play under the wild cherry tree,
Getting drunk on the berries,
Press our feet into the dry dirt
Until the sun moves beyond us,
And the shade disappears into evening.
It will be time to gather things in,
Latching up for night – the time for washing feet,
To listen for the old truck coughing
Out of the distance on quiet wheels,
Bringing folks back from the orchards,
Ashy folks, their faces
Stinging from peach fuzz.

Home is Where

THESE BONES ARE POEMS

Moonlight in the trees.
I hug my knees.
Soft cotton trousers wrinkle in my hands, on my legs,
My haunches on a tree stump.

Like a sea gull, I think, on this piece of wood,
Except that I am land locked,
Nowhere near the water.

A tree was felled here in the name of culling,
Clear in the moonlight pieces dead and dying.
It was itself whole once.

Those still standing waver in the light.
Clouds move over shadow, silver cast.
Living trees become invisible.
Perhaps I am a seagull perched on the edge of infinite black.
That is the sea here, that is the sea, I think.

These days lines of lost poetry are beached like dead whales on the damp
    sands of
my mind, bones of poems, some from my mind, some from others.

Bones should have funerals,
Gathered with respect and care before we carry them away.
A funeral should have ceremony.
Ceremony before fire, ceremony before the machine that chews two
    wood chips.
Some honoring of green and gold, remembrance of the faithful tolerance
    of ice and rain.

I smell what's coming, move deliberately.
The more I push and shove the more I wonder why is death so heavy?
How often have I been cut down, cut up and moved around?
How often have I sniffed the rain and heard the threat of storm and still,
    still lift my arms

and flail at the wind?

My hands are sore but I will only know this later when I finish
stacking wood.
Witness this.
These bones are poems, left on the dark shore of space for anyone to find.
I move deliberately in honor of what is.
Rain is here.
The earth aroma fills my head.

DONNY HATHAWAY

1945-1979

listening to "He Ain't Heavy, He's My Brother"

Lingering at the edge
of want, grasping how,
clawing, gripping again,
then leaping, spread-winged,
shape of wail, taking yes
to good night. Rivering,
ghosting in a slow-drag:
churching gravity. Praise
armed to hold bones, larynx
of soldered gold, soldier
for the blues coup, heaven
flung, for what's coursing out.
Past the plunge of need, of we,
when salt-throat bears all
to the blood of undone.

LIGHTSKINNED ID

for Neruda, for The South

It so happens my id is red.
Check the clues—my lightskinned
parts: underneath my underwear,
if you pull the skin taut; on the white
hand side and down my wrist
where the veins branch out
like green pipes; my foot-bottom
and almost my eyes up close. It used
to be my whole self, until I was
six for sure. But a brownness
took over. Started swimming
at nine, how sun and chlorine
kissed the night into my skin.
There was no turning back.

But my id is good
and redboned. Like slicing open
a pear for the surprise
of its flesh. Look hard:
there's a murmur of bronze
in my skin. I'm a peanut-butter oreo,
an apple dipped in molasses;
I'm a broad dish of crème brûlée.
O the chiaroscuro of my self.

Still not freed from Freud, I'm fried
on the outside. What a brown on me!
Since the color beneath my color
is curried. It wants to come out,
my high yellow id. Always on the verge
of beige. It wants me to Ambi my skin,
to blossom peach all over. My id has such
a need. Here it goes with its libido of gold,
clashing with the ego, my I, a browner negro,

Home is Where

and the superego, who's a radiant absence
of white. He thinks he's in charge.

It makes me act like I'm
better than people, my id. It wants
what it wants. It makes me lick
melted margarine and steal copper
coins from bums. Makes me
bathe in mango juice. Pour sour
milk down my ears and sign
checks in blood to prove it.
On the forms I fill in
Other and scribble *Yellow*
on the inside in red ink.
I suck the nectar beneath my skin.

My id's pretty niggerish
(for a mulatto). My id is everyone's
Indian uncle. It's taking me
to Hollywood on an undersong
of cream. My id is colourstruck
with itself. My id is El DeBarge.
My id; its job is to keep it light.
How my id misses the eighties.

If only this amber
at heart were enough.

I have to praise it. I have to lull it
with new roses. Run my fingers
along this sallow river
of desire. Stuck in the plantation
kitchen, black ants dying
in an orgy of honey.

CARNIVAL NIGHT AT SHADOW WALL

After "Bethe Saar Shadow with bubble Wall"
By Laurel Canyon 1988

There is a picture show
At Shadow Wall tonight
Reruns of 1935
Carnival night, again
Booming
All around us
Bright color tents like squatters scattered across
An endless stretch of heaven

To the right
Seven black forget-me-not's
Stand pressed against the rails
Their Snow White
next to them.

The truth about the South lies in the
Ease in which the Bible belt
Can be taken off and put on at will.

It didn't bother anyone's spirit
To throw stones at mama
All God's children should not be black
If your skin is white.

When papas' headlights
Broke the darkness

We all knew
would never cross the fair grounds that night,
or taste a single sweet confection.

Papa
as black as the face of Bassett, at midnight

Home is Where

Would beat our asses
till our eyes bled
Now that he caught us

The night was his life
Not ours

Mama said "we were what a poor man fell back on,"
when "all else" was drawing its last breathe.

Nothing more.

I never knew what happened next
The truth is like a shadow sometimes
casting it's uncertain light
over all of our lives

Papa's anger
As hot as the steam rising from the streets in hell,
began to choke the air around us
With terrifying resolve.

I felt mama turn away from us hard,
Then papa was falling
Falling like the great trees in the forest behind our shack.

They said that it was an accident later.

There were no witnesses at Shadow Wall
To speak for papa.

Forty years later our tongues are still too numb
To utter the words
that want to be said.

Our mama was a murderer.

LOVE WIFE

Alzheimer's has my father right now

So he can't remember who my son is

Or

What happened to his little blue Dodge
he wrapped around a tree one night
two hours from no where in particular.

A crooked cardboard note
Taped to the back door reads:

Please do not go out
without me.
Love Wife

No sweet Guyanese voice next door, anymore
calling out the window:

Grandfather! Grandfather!
Why are you outside alone....?

Go back in side!
Go back–

inside.

Home is Where

UNCLE COLUMBUS

You are the tallest tree in this photograph
the yellow-brown saplings colored in sepia spray.

They all looked up to you–they thought
you would have brought them, with you to college.

Forty-two, the numbers that promised a way
out of roach infested factories and carcinogen

pumping plants, that promised three generations
much of all they had. The novice new man

would be first to trail cobblestone walkways
and one of the first to have a white man

look their way, not to beat them from distrust
or contempt. It was hard to see disconcerting

winds in your own sky but you continued to propel
against meager propensities, far above the stratosphere.

Each branch climbed higher and some storms and
man-made forces wanted to prune even the healthy ones

or have you carry its debris as you continued on
your marvelous feet. Proud: you could see

laughing lineage wonder would their
dreams reach your Swannanoa sky.

CHARLOTTE HAWKINS BROWN CINQUAINS

Premonition
1898

Charlotte's meeting with Alice Freeman Palmer

Cambridge
The place of dance
opus stirring jewel
onyx-ochre vernal clad minds
release

My calling is ...

Teacher
of Sedalia
peeling world in front eyes
roam remote of their window's gait
further

Commencement
Carrie Esther Totten Strother, 1930

Waiting
white in flair—girl
No more, in blaze of white
backdrop of black and white tableau
contrast

Home is Where

A CONVERSATION

James Madison University at Festival Center
June 18, 2009

For Nikky Finney

"...pay attention to what sits inside yourself and watches you"
                                        Lucille Clifton

I watched two women
 not a world's distance
Maybe a minor fissure
 quarter lifetimes.
She, mother-poet, saw herself as
The girl with braids, the color of rain.
Those eyes looking back to her daughter
 witnessed her imaginings
 Taller.
Mother, revealing her tangible self
 inextricable map
Left for chartering strangers, fans, voices, to walk

walking—all who admired.
This same woman
This same audience walked with you
 first job into a shoe store, to Howard, outside
 the Shenandoah Valley with her—
Now, we are in "Jeopardy"
A champion marveled
Gallant we are.
Laughing but crying within, inhaling our angst
 Judgment
has trailed us to our doorsteps, in school
every street light   store
Corner cul-de-sac. Listening to the voices
As we kiss the winds. You tell us we've always
Been erudite, glowing gems of many—

guarded secret minds, as if clandestine.
　See us.　See us
How radiant, remarkable we are—
How graceful and gregarious we are.
　　　　Intrepid through the work and minds prominent and
nameless bones
This one good woman reminds us all, as if we forgot

TRUE MASTER

"Who's the baddest low down, mofo round this town?"
-Sho Nuff, The Last Dragon

Imagine Kwai Chang Caine
As a four foot eleven black woman
Gray hair, gold rimmed glasses
But not as stiff as David Carradine
Imagine Gordon Lui
In the 36 chambers
With a big black pocket book
Instead of a three section staff
Grandma moved her energy from the ground up
She practiced in house dresses and stockings in
Gum bottom Reeboks
Her empty hand techniques were pinches
To ears and palm strikes to bottoms
Her kitchen broom style was lethal
Lightning,
Yellow straw descending
Too fast to duck
Only matched by her green switch form
Swung Bruce Lee quick
She cultivated her chi with collards and cornbread
She meditated in a lazy-boy
Her glasses just at the tip of her nose
A National Enquirer in her lap
Her Kung Fu grip held my hand
When we crossed busy streets
She told us that the Manchus
(Or republicans) were not to be trusted
Under any conditions
And democrats, only as far as you could throw them
At age 82 she walked through a group of
Teenagers with skateboards and painful piercings
Daring them to stand in her way
A gallon of milk in her right hand

Cocked like a Jet-Li sidekick
The crowd made way for the master
In annals of Shaolin this is called:
The Battle For The Harris Teeter Parking Lot.

CALL OF DUTY

My wife's womb is a world
My son lives inside
At night I sing him his ABC's
I want him to talk early
I place head phones on my
Wife's belly and play 90's hip hop
I think about holding him and rocking
Him to sleep with Wu Tang instrumentals
I think of the things I need to teach him
The man lessons, the Blackman survival
In America lessons
I hope he will listen better than I did
I wish my father were here to help me
I said ten fingers and ten toes
Healthy baby, when people asked me
Did I want a boy or a girl?
But I prayed for a son
Now I pray to get the father hood thing right
I pray and I pray that I won't fuck it up

THE ECONOMIES

Shana sells crack out of a blue coffee can
And braids hair in a kitchen with no heat
Five dollars for corn rolls straight to the back
Ten dollars for designs, zigzags, and such
Nimble fingers dip in green grease
Lubricate wooly heads
Braids tight enough to make
Her clients look Blackaneese
It's all bidness
Hands on hips holding fine tooth comb
Explaining how Jay-Z use to sell China White
Now he got him a Beyonce'
Now he producing Broadway Plays
Now he sitting up close at the Inauguration
With a fur hat on
She gonna open a chain of hair braiding salons
Once that crack money stack up
Braid rich people hair like Iverson
Joe Kennedy sold liquor made his son president
She saw it on A&E
3 knocks at the back door for wide eyed zombie flesh respite
This ain't for everybody, but neither is being paid, she says
Smile as wide as the American flag dangling from her key chain

MAMI WATA

can't wait
don't wanna wait
tired of waiting
wanna jump in
swim
like Mami Wata
become
Deity
of your African waters
wanna
become one
with moon
sun
sky
grasp the shore of your existence
and pull you in

A CONFLAGRATION OF THE SCALP

Sittin' in a chair
at the Total Hair Care
head immersed in the shampoo bowl
listening to the screams.
You must have been scratchin' girl!
As she shouts for her momma or her grannie
to rescue her from chemical warfare
going on in the curls of a little girl
Toes curlin' up
Nails diggin' in to the skin of the shampoo girl
for moral support
like she was holdin' on to the hand of her man
during a contraction
Yelpin' for a hose to extinguish blazing flames
but wanting more than that,
the extinction of nappiness
and the evolution of smooth
silky silky soul sheen
of flowing beauty queens
flyin' farrah-fawcett-free
flippin' bangs out of her face.
Straight.
As straight as a priest molesting little boys
trying to be something he's not
Or was it his dad who wanted him not
to want another man?
Or was it her mom who couldn't withstand
the comb breaking in her hand?

That girl had to have been scratchin'!
Scratchin' like four little girls
on their way to Sunday school
one morning in September?
Opening up pores
for white cream
to burn brown scalp

like white hooded robes
burning churches in Birmingham
Screams continuing
Black women waiting for hours on end
Like getting our hair done
was our second part time job
Workin' overtime
gettin' paid way above minimum wage
gettin' paid with waves for days and days
Shirley temple curls
Twisted mountainous sculptures
of red purple blue blond weaves
cascading down like streams
and piled high like pyramids
Egyptian Queens talkin' about,
Oooh this humidity is terrible on my hair
My bills ain't been paid, but they can wait
'cause my 'do has got to be laid!
And *I* over here spending
my last dime to avoid a frizzy new growth hair line
reminding me of the time
I finally learned how to drive
a car with a manual transmission
My sister had been unsuccessfully
teaching me for weeks
but I had a hot date that night
I had to look tight
Her 1979 Honda Civic
had been sitting in the driveway for days
She was away on tour,
and I had a hair appointment.
Determined, I fumbled to find the ignition
The clutch popped
and I jerked all the way up to the beauty shop
Rolling backwards at every stop
Getting my hair done transcended my fear
of learning how to drive a stick
Vanity was my driving force,

my Hoke chauffeuring me like Miss Daisy
up Oakland hills and through Berkeley traffic.
Put-puttin' the last mile back to my street—
but my hair was lookin' as sweet
as homemade pumpkin pie
arriving in one sumptuous piece.

I have been able to drive any
manual transmission standard stick shift
ever since.

THINGS MY FATHER TAUGHT ME

The back porch. The cock
& pump: two for a light
kickback–the bb grazes
the pine pole before it jumps
to earth. Four or more–
If straight shoot–I add
My signature to it–lead
Pellets in the belly of an old
Tree-turned-phone pole,
& my father's congratulations.
Daddy says, Don't think
About the pain, keep
The left hand level. On
The barrel, my left palm
Holds the weight, holds
This weapon inscribed
With my initials;
The delta of my right
Shoulder & budding
Breasts keep everything
In line. I reach
For the trigger's tight tongue
To hold, flick. I pull back, move
The one opened eye right
To see clearly As the shadowed
Aperture moves left.
The telephone pole's
silver-dollar label
Caught in crosshairs.

SHORN

I've pulled away the browning leaves to save the tree; sacrificed
A whole limb for the trunk. When gangrene threatened
My great-grandmother's right leg, doctors had to amputate
Everything below the knee.

Outside, in South Carolina, my grandfather's work shed
Is covered in kudzu. If I lived there still, I would cut back
The years of leaves, would let the light back
Into the windows, would save the wood planks
Nailed together by hand from rot.

But I am in my bathroom taking scissors
To dreadlocked hair, exposing my neck and torso. Now, I am
All face and cheekbones, all neck and stretch marks
Cross-hatching my collarbones.

After I cut the dead leaves, I returned them to the base
Of the tree. For my hair, there is no equivalent.

PARADISE HELL BACK

Step on the block
Step one, step two, step three
Step to the top of the slave auctions block
The clock is tickin, tic toc, tic toc, tic toc

Spread your legs
Raise your arms
Split your lips, top, bottom, up and down you know what I mean
They stare and wonder of how many left
That is eggs,
Can she breed

Lift her titties where milk resides,
Make a mockery of sagging glands
Milk they care none of for storage or such
Groping and poking and squeeze with their hands
They claim hate and market her product
To lay un-consensual at night in sheds

Pretendin pride lays in the crevices of our privates
They rape and attempt to scrape the pathogens of our streams of
    being
Silencing tunnels of consummation to bare chocolate seeds
Simply to get slaps on the wrists that hey this is just the common
    courtesy of a white southerner's good deeds
Slave woman's paradise of hell she feels
Hoping and praying she'd be freed from pits
Praying and crying and pleading are deals
She and she made like praying addicts
Maybe da lawd will have mercy and grant me appeal

For being black
For being poe
For being fat
For being soe

For being young
For being piccaninnie
For being old
For being aunt jemimah and dear old mammie
Jiggaboo, coon, colored and nigga too

File my appeal
Sho hope tha jury be in
To decide my fate
From the infamous and infinite sheer practice of HATE.

RHYTHM OF OUR BOXES

for the Women of Women of Women before us

It is to which life began and exits at genesis
Caves of hidden stories, testimonies differing from one to another,
Yet, in different comparisons.

Foreshadowing legends of how we came to be of
Such authentic structure
Identified as deformity and gawked as pleasurably.

We, unknowingly spread legs of innocence
For acceptance, for change, for chance,
At being of the normal kind.

We walk with tempos that our boxes harmonize rhythms only our
hips sway to

Bumps like gelatin mold, we stride with our own orchestra in each
step.

Stepping into our past of oddity, we
Lay bones, in tombs, cases, and museums
Of examination as anatomy, today, TOO
Dissecting body and spirit of opened legs
Speculated by those thought and perceived to
Be medical geniuses.

We, be exhibits of un-respected art as
Muscular dissected models in Anatomy and Physiology 212 section 04.

They peel layers of our boxes as rose petals with daggers stating,
"is she OR is she NOT a *freak*"?

Here, we the Black female species pigmented with shades of kikawah
    beans, caramel
and mocha created with abstract features by God,

Stand as opening acts, featured acts, afraid of curtains pulling, the
    crowd
Oooooooooooooooooooohhing and aaaaaaaaahhing,
As they announce the excitement, the astonishing
Rhythm of OUR Boxes.

BRIMMING

After "Waccamaw #28" by Brian Rutemberg

A silken veil, this light rain
softens the flaming oak leaves.

The tarmac is gleaming wet.
God on the black river's belly.

Deep at night, the rain lifts,
a cool breeze tickles my skin.

Sweat and soft warm dew's mist.
Naked, I slip through the woods.

A new fist of cloud crowds the west,
I stand, head back and open-mouthed.

GRAVES

After "Irish Painting #15" by Brian Rutemberg

After the light colored shallows,
the deep river is our resting place.

We plunge into the chill,
everything is black down here.

Staring upwards, the sky
glows in mists of green and silver.

Below the river bed undulates
like a drought-burnt prairie.

Deeper, the smooth shoulder
of a sudden valley glows yellow.

We find the skulls of simple folk
buried in the broken graveyard

on the slopes of a village
lost to the floodwaters of a trained

river, we find a brick crucifix.
and the sound of prayers murmuring

in the dark belly of this river.
When we come up for air

the boat has drifted far down
stream, and a soft rain is falling.

CAROLINA GOLD

After "Carolina Gold" by Brian Rutemberg

Hurl me though memory
and I will return panting
with my satchel filled
with the stories strangers
tell me at the crossroads.

Here in the low country
it takes just a few years
for a storm's scars to heal,
for the moss and thickets
to cover crumbled stones.

Here in the low country
a forest covers multitude
of sins, and we make camp
humming, trying not to hear
the clamor underfoot.

If you walk barefoot
through the forest, you will
feel the dip and swell
of old graves. How near
the surface is the water table.

Words like "beauty"
are the artist's hope, but
his dreams are of terror
and the testing of light–
the language of color.

I walk thorough this hall
and find myself tossed
from light to light,
and it is hard to breathe,

hard to stop to look.
Outside, the sudden light
of Columbia in July
is strange comfort.
I make blood poems
before I sleep.

THE GRILL MASTER

Southerners are used to heat lightning.
The flash of light that arrives thunderless,
but resembles a javelin splitting
the sky in half.
Northerners don't have
this sort of weather;
but I can feel it
threatening miles away.
It is an unspoken thought
spooking the sky when
we pull up in the jagged gravel
of Churchill's bar.
My Jewish friend Hiram bolts out the car,
inquires about the chickens roasting
on the grill and the PBR cans
lined up on the wall like sinners
approaching the guillotine.
When the grill master's hazel eyes
sight my brown skin he barks at Hiram
"you ain't from around here, are ya boy?"
His twang dismissing me, digging me
an instant grave as the flash
suddenly darts across the dusky sky.
Living in the South requires understanding
of heat lightning completely.
Those pre-warnings of an approaching storm
cast down like weapons,
cast down like the dictionary derivative of javelin
the old French's *javeline*
the dimunitive of *javelot*
meaning spear,
a weapon cast by hand
its stinging silence heard oh so loudly
whizzing past my ears.

MY LAST DAY AT HOLY CROSS

Outside the school they argued as the sun danced
on black asphalt. Momma's nostrils flared as she spoke
to the nun in short staccato phrases. *But she's not stupid.*
Sometimes she gets flustered. At age six, flustered didn't compute
but I knew my troubled tongue was the problem. When reading
those Nan and Ted sentences stuck in my mouth like grains of salt,
clogged in a shaker that fell out in clumps, or sometimes not at all.
But this stutterer listened close until Miss Mary Mack,
complete with her white collar, said things I did understand. *She's holding*
back the rest of class. Perhaps she should stay behind. Her voice chilled
with ice cubes while momma stayed hot as a furnace. And mostly,
I stood—my mouth buttoned shut—the same way I learned ballet.
My brown feet posed in some strange configuration, arms open,
slightly bent at the elbows as if asking for a hug. This is how I learned
every stance; how I learned my positions.

Home is Where

JAZZ FORMULA

Take the spirited voices of Congo Square
The tickling of ebony and ivory pairs
The rhythmic heartbeat of bass and drum
Add the wail of sax, and then simmer to a hum.

What is this delightful brew
Full of souls, old and new?

It's a lonely lover's croon
The swing of jazz
A single lady's anthem
Lots of razz-ma-tazz.

THERE EXIST SOME X

1

The killer is in the house.
Six words.
Two nouns.
Two definite articles.
One verb.
One preposition.
Infinite meanings.
There is some house
and in it
there is a killer, but
not just any, but
the killer in *the*
house, yes, that
house and that
killer, who
perhaps is no
killer at all, but
a handsome woman,
a beautiful man,
a choice turn of phrase,
a dream and
the *house* is
my head, my world,
and of course
is is ironic.

Home is Where

2

That house
and that killer
on that block
of that street
in that city
in that culture
where irony is not salvation, but only salve

3

wear
highrony
kiss
nut
salvation

PROCESS

1

The ritual of making
dies upon completion.

The body remembers,
like making love.

The body remembers
the gestures,

the midair changes,
the fall of an arm,

the angle of approach,
of withdrawal.

A calligraphy
survives completion,

but the making
is long long done.

2

The midair
changes
are the
tough
ones.

Catch me
before
I release,
if you please,
can.

3

eye
raylease

THE BODY OF LUCILLE

The job of the artist is not to leave you where she found you.
—Lucille Clifton, American poet

the body of lucille roosted
in the body of thelma,

her life nestled
to the feathery lap of mama,

who wore twelve fingers
(while whispering Dunbar)

just as she wore twelve,
just as the baby growing inside
of her would wear twelve.

lucille saw things,
and lived her light-filled life

from her daughter-roost,
dying on the same day
her mama died,

fifty years ahead, now, the daughters
& sons who as instructed, *left the movies,*

join all the poets in Babylon,
who once believed
their lives merely *ordinary,*

each of us now, holding out our red
calla lily hands, counting out our fingers
to be sure, humming now, longing now,
forever, for the two-headed body of lucille.

Home is Where

WINDOW IN THE WINDOW

Inspired by a painting of Christopher Myers

It's always the same.
She raises the window,
studies the street, then disappears.
She comes back with a stool, a worn wooden one.
She sits so still people on the street
don't even notice her nor that moment
when a person can be where they are not,
where they can
imagine
even when everything around them is loud and red
and purple and people are busy getting
where they are going and chaps are yelling
back and forth while horns blow cusses and
music.
It must be nice to feel the yellow of the sun
and forget the food that needs cooking, forget
the dishes that need washing, forget
the kids that need teaching,
floors that need scrubbing
the man that needs loving,
and the woman he's been seeing.
And ain't it something how easy
he goes to her and then comes home,
as easy as blood traveling
back through the heart.
How he kisses her at the door
and she is forced not to smell him.
No,
she is forgetting the girl,
who lived on the 12th floor,
the one with more dreams than talent.
The one that married a man
like her man, the kind that offers a wicked love
the kind you can't and won't live without

but one morning that girl stepped outside
the window and off the earth.
Or better yet, the woman in the window
is just feeling the breeze
and how nice it is to have time to think
on how some things are always the same.

HOW JOURNEYS BEGIN

*"Women have sat indoor all these millions of years, so that by this
time, the very walls are permeated by their creative force, which has,
indeed so overcharged the capacity of bricks and mortar that it must
needs harness itself to pens and brushes and business and politics."*
                                                        –Virginia Woolf

She sits
her face
as placid
as a pool of water.
Her breath leaks
out and struggles
to enter back in.
Through a tiny
window,
she can see
the world parade
by with its banners
and drums and singers...
and they are all dancing to a tune
that doesn't make sense.

She feels
something tumbling
through her,
it is the blood trudging
back through her heart.
She turns
her head as if
listening to some call.
There is something that she
must say, some things that she
must do.

Her fingers
grip the chair,
tearing the flowery fabric.

Her arms like rusty levers
left her up.
Over the tile floor,
her right foot is poised
pointed and aimed.
When she levels
it, foundations crack,
walls crumble,
and reins are loosed.

ENGLISH

Sometimes
I think it is not my language,
not my first language.
The sounds are unyielding,
like metal on my tongue,
a bit in my mouth.
I cannot shape the words
I need to say,
the adjectives are too weak,
adverbs do not add enough.
The words get across the meaning
but not the feel of a thing,
none of its texture.
What I mean to say is...

Perhaps,
I have another language,
one that I can sing in,
the one that I forgot.
If it is true that blood
holds memory,
perhaps my true language is still
with me, trapped in my subconscious.
If I listen, listen careful to some African
student or at some Pow-Pow
perhaps it will come to me.
If I pray right,
maybe my spirit will be loosened
and I'll sing
in tongues.

daughters of this dust

i

feeling real good
big boned
mahogany ass shelf
indigo left eye
same eye grandma found
rolling around in the cat's bowl
i teach geometry from unshaven armpits
geography begins between my toes
five different patois sing your name backwards.

ii

dawn colors my back mauve
you mistake it for argentina
shipwrecked soul
you pierce me with the knives of hunger
i cry a shark's song
for the loneliness at the bottom
of your eyes.

iii

your palms peel back my eyes
and stone the devils
living there.

iv

only you believed the blue eye
when she said she swam with mermaids
danced calypso beneath the sand
removed oshun curses.

Home is Where

v

feeling real good
impregnating condensed light
weaving new pigmentation
into right eye.

waiting for love

alone cold mint tea in orange plastic torn djelaba a red you forbid waiting drowning
in six too many capsules of magic trying to remember the words of the astrologer or
what you were screaming as you fled into the secret clay wall of your brother's
house trying to understand that i am only allowed to pray on wednesdays pray only
in the blue mosque in Mazar-e-Sharif or join your sisters at Karte-e-Shakhi this
strange but magical Kabul my captor Kabul the first time i drank the darkness of a
particular Pashtun male the morning i am face to face with Malalai the only female
police in Kandahar we play burqua eye games before she slaps me shouting to
lower my gaze cover my hennaed wrists or wake up dead i return to these walls i
name home to the sacred stitches and colors rugs from your tribe my dowry my art
i smoke the ancient hashish i found buried beneath the kitchen wall tiles your
youngest sister Selah arrives tells me it belonged to your grandmother we smoke
sleep cry eat the feta olives grapes and dream of weddings hair beaches nail polish
dark warriors bearing Tibetan music we arrive by caravan to the wedding site your
father tells me you will come so i search for you amongst the men that encircle the
wedding party and begin wishing that i could place a hidden camera in the back of
my burqua so i can see you when you remain invisible i am the foreign woman
laughing undetected beneath my blue wedding tent a gift from your mother
reminding me that this is the way for a refugee wife suddenly i smell the secret
blend of wedding oils against my face it is Zarah your sister laughing far too openly
amongst men hugging thanking me for her happiness not understanding the smile
in her eyes i do not feel my body shift or her left hand seize the gun from my pocket Zar
my sister-in-law forced to marry the man with green teeth shoots her head off
during the beginning of the weeklong Eid-e-Ghorbon trying to forget all i am forced
to remember razor wire nights Koochie boys wearing desert faces speaking to me in
all the languages of hunger begging for gold thread i don't remember the name of
the particular dark Pashtun male or the color of Zarah's wedding dress i try to forget
her smile the way blood creates its own art spraying the cake the gifts of sugar
bread honey spices prayer carpets scarves from her sisters i remember your daily
screams when i forgot and opened the door to visitors in Peshawar forgetting
always to wear my chador i remind you that i am the same woman who raced
barefoot escaping the war rapes of sixty Russians behind a hill in Wazir Akbu Khan i
am the woman you danced with beneath the stars in Kandahar the same astrologer
who meets your eyes in the bazaar i am every woman in the snow covered streets of Gh
or in Herat Province lighting candles in search of Zarah's gold teeth i am the
lost bullet lodged in the wedding cake that the man with green teeth serves to his

Home is Where

new bride Fatima i will meet her in the bathroom stalls next door to the blue mosque and pretend i do not see her tap my market basket remove the muslin cloth covering the fresh chicken dates onions potatoes lemons drop my knife into the deep pockets of her riding skirts our smiles whispering salaams it is the coldest night without you and i am preparing a dinner for your return the foods of our passionate longings lentil and bulgur patties stuffed eggplant kasseri cheese my brother smuggles from Turkey chicken pilaf raisin compote i spend hours shaving oiling my skin soaking in frankincense ginger jasmine water arrange rose petals throughout our bed sharpen candle sticks that will light this night there is no more hashish guns or knives only the wedding feast waiting.

feeding the light

for aunt lilly
(who taught me how to see in the dark)

we risk ice storms postpone passionate death to swirl head first beyond wise
breathing lessons beyond crimson soaked necks crushed knuckles and stinking
birth skin all the way down past gray fields chaste moons yet light so pregnant it
seeps across insolent skies too ashamed to name the dances too ashamed to name
the shaman who eats the jazz behind iron doors praying for half notes that cure
blindness cure the bestial that lurks inside places troubles on the water one tenor
eyelash at a time reappearing at the bottom of a worn out morning after cup of mil
pharoah herbie ornette we risk falling out of the well used belly the platinum
engraved womb that cherishes a right handed bass player clean blue velvet shoes
that keeps nameless eyes waiting he has a way of singing thick thighs apart in the
middle of blazing duets knows how to pull blossoms out of the ground through
february snow drifts feeds a bastard sky child nothing but horn a wild child reading
the book of the thousand nights and night blue velvet shoes can't keep a damn lie
straight in between identifying frozen crushed faces slaughtered for whispering jaz
slaughtered for smelling like jazz wooden zulu spears silver coins wet feathers we
risk losing our sense of flight our gypsy hearts in search of jazz eating shaman who
serves holy bread with blues water his voice slicing daylight feeding small pieces to
all that is left of a brown jungle girl whose bones smoke up every juke joint in
between here and all the places she died alone on alabaster steps voice strangled b
kisses prayers abandoned weeping shaman cures her dreams pours billie sarah nir
ella down her throat horny hips thrust shatter shred blue velvet shoes across the
room a narrow mirror becomes a road and she learns to fly straight through a glas
sky she be music now she be night-fed she be forgiveness rupturing a worn out
morning after cup of herself she be birthing and remixing clocks calendars numbe
maps her sweat sweet with round midnight honey washing up onto a shore of
seasons smelling like drums tasting like a flute of curry we risk the night searching
wanting to taste her skin.

I JUST WANT TO LOOK

A friend called to tell me there was a topless woman picketing
outside the court house so I got my keys and eyeglasses,
but when I arrived, there were already so many onlookers,
I could see nothing but the top of her sign reading:
I HAVE THE RIGHT TO—the rest of it was blocked
by bobble-headed men in suits, by near boys in ball caps,
by afros and bald spots. "What does it say?" I asked the mail-
man fanning himself with a big confidential looking envelope.
"I'm sorry," he said, then "This is for you," handing me
an envelope that had nothing but "To son" "From Mom"
written on it. The crowd moved a foot or two east, then
a foot or two west following the bare sign bearing woman.
"I know I should have given it to you long ago," the mailman
was saying, "but I just couldn't bear being the bearer of bad news
another day." "That's what you think," a large woman yelled down
in the direction of the topless woman from the second floor
of the court house tossing out what looked like an old jacket.
The men sent a disapproving roar up and the jacket seemed
to gather wind and flap off toward the river. "You have no idea
how hard my job is," the mail man said below the ruckus,
something was going on at the steps of the court house.
"Is she dressing now" I asked a policeman fondling his nightstick.
"You're lucky," he said and I thought maybe he knew how I'd stopped
less than an inch from the kneecaps of an old lady pedestrian
that morning. "Your name is Lucky Jefferson, correct?
The infamous numbers runner and star pimp of Garfield?"
"No, no, I don't know what you're talking about," I said.
"And there is never anything in my own mailbox," the mail man
sobbed to me. It was like a dark forest there in the middle
of downtown, all that shoulder to shouldering and gawking
at backs. The policeman stared at me and said "I'm sure
you're Lucky. We were in high school together. Remember the night
We listened to *Purple Rain* until my mother got home
from her job at the hospital?" "Rick," I said. "Is that you?
Lord, I never thought you'd become a cop!" "My name is Alvin,"
the policeman said reaching for his cuffs. Inside the envelope

the mail man gave me I found a drawing of daisies in a blue vase,
and below them the words: *You forgot Mother's Day, Bastard.*
"Woooo!" the crowd said, but I still could see nothing
of the topless woman. "I send my mother cards, but she sends nothing
to me," the mailman said. The policeman placed a hand on his shoulder.
The woman from the second floor of the courthouse yelled
"No, no you don't have the right to do that!" and I realized, suddenly,
she was talking to me. I lifted the empty envelope over my head
and I swear everyone in the crowd turned to face me.

Home is Where

ODE TO BIG TREND

Pretty soon the Negroes were looking to get paid.
My partner, Big Trend, wiped his ox neck and said

He wasn't going to wait too much longer. You
Know that look your daddy gets before he whups you?

That's how Big Trend looked. There was a pink scar
Middling his forehead. Most people assumed a bear

Like him couldn't read anything but a dollar.
But I'd seen him napping so I knew he held more

Than power in those hands. They could tear
A Bible in two. Sometimes on the walk home I'd hear

Him reciting poems. But come Friday, he was the one
The fellas asked to speak to the boss. He'd go alone,

Usually, and we imagined the boss buckled
Into his shadow because our money always followed.

A. MACHINE

Hey, I am learning what it means to ride condemned.
I may be breaking up. I am doing 85 outside the kingdom

Of heaven, under the overpass and passed over,
The past is over and I'm over the past. My odometer

Is broken, can you help me? When you get this mess-
Age, I may be a half ton crush, a half tone of mist

And mystery, maybe trooper bait with the ambulance
Ambling somewhere, or a dial of holy stations, a band-

Age of clamor and spooling, a dash and semaphore,
A pupil of motion on my way to be buried or planted or

Crammed or creamed, treading light and water or tread
And trepidation, maybe. Hey, I am backfiring along a road

Though the future, *I am alive* skidding on the tongue,
When you get this message, will you sigh, *My lover is gone*?

AN UNEXPECTED LIFT

Wind is what I'll remember,

not the speed of rolling downhill,
or my legs dangling off the side of the bike.
I'll remember wind—
wanting to loose my hair to it,
fear keeping my hands fast to the handlebars.
Maybe I'll remember Aldo's arms
pushing against my body,
the sound of his laughter
as I began to laugh,
and how there was no smell to any of it.

SALIK

His house sits by the river.
Tightly woven palm fronds cover the sky,
and a raised floor keeps the mud out.

I am watching the river,
and he is watching me,
his hands nervously rubbing his knees.

He reaches for his cigarettes,
and tells me that when high tide comes
you can feel the river through the floor boards.

He takes off his shirt
and shows me his dragon tattoo—
a scrawl of black and gray across his back.

I reach out to touch it,
but it is too unfinished, too raw.
I put my hands in my lap.

We both watch the river
rising higher and higher.
A woman nearby begins to sing.

FIVE DAYS TO DIE

Day 1
I'm sure it will rain.
Rain always comes after bad news.
But, I have always loved the rain.
On the first day, I will sit outside in the rain,
let it soak my skin,
and remember all the things
I did not do.

Day 2
I will wake up late,
my bones will ache,
and I will not know where I am.
I will touch things
as if they, too, have betrayed me.
And then I'll open a door.
I'll go out and look for things.
I'll start with shiny things—
shards of glass and lost earrings.
Maybe I'll end up on a doorstep.
Maybe it will belong to a friend.
It won't matter.
There is nothing can be done anyway.

Day 3
You will find me
curled up in your rocking chair.
You won't ask me anything,
just cover me with that blanket I like,
and go about your day.
You know, but say nothing.

Day 4
We sit drinking tea,
and you count the hours,
while I think of how long it's been
since I was held, kissed, and gently opened.
I am not waiting for anything,
only knowing that there is
so much more to be done.

Day 5
Memory is a fickle thing.
I remember red and warmth.
I remember hearing the ocean.
I remember thinking of faces
that were not there.
I remember holding my hand out,
and then pulling it away.
I remember the sting of living alone.
I remember the tune of a song,
but the words have left me.

MOTHER

The angled curve of her shoulder
molded
Smooth and worn
Oiled to the pores
A catcher's mit to her daughters' foreheads
A well in her armpit deep
enough
She was
enough
for them
Her misguided attempts at womanhood are there
Behind their irises
Mutated blooms
Reminding her of an ego
Now muffled under sound
youngest Swahili princess screaming
Frustrated cries
edging her toddling hips on pine
dying to step up and swing
The creases in her neck resemble stump rings
Marking her years in the wilderness
Her worth waving on the other side of the river in which she's wading
ever so careful
can't be swept away again
bones barely healed from the last time white water split her
Sent her spinning
like pulp wood into a highway ditch
can't swing her arms wide enough to wipe dust off anymore
She's settled in
her names
Mother   Ma   Mama   Muh   Nana
suckling on her spirit
they absorb her tears and feed
her compassion
They speak to her in nuanced innuendo
Deciphering codes of silent crushed ego

Humble the walk
Blessed her soul
Content her goal
Mother

GENERAL SONIA

for Sonia Sanchez

Words get stuck stuttering   stuttering   stuttering
whisping so fast soaring by   bye   bye
your white tongue
Pure...clean...honest...brutal...now

Marking yourself with ink
blue black from brown blood
and we are in awe that you let us stand and watch you bleed

Tell it, it's told
Spread it so bold
Purely me
You have sewn seed for me to breathe
pure...clean...honest...brutal...now

I take assignment from you General Sonia
for you challenge me to be me, unapologetically
unwavering...un, un, un, excusable

Make me work for my words for I need them to
breathe breath into my children's ears
in whispers I shout to them, whilst crying out to you about love...
    pain
pure...clean...honest...brutal...now

I pass my pen across the page with ink
blue black from brown blood
seeping slowly from the blisters of your fingers and the cracks of
    your lips

your life pours out down your breasts and feeds me songs of fire
I catch it, it runs hot from my hands across the page you are my sage
    to burn
pure...clean...honest...brutal...now

My allegiance to you carries a torch filled with burnt discarded
poems that never had a chance to bleed drops of renaissance wisdom

I am a child you are rearing over the microphone and I have no
choice but to raise myself up to your call...

And even if you never lay your soul-stirring eyes on me again

I carry you...for me
General Sonia

-Selah

"QUE SERA SERA"

In my car, driving through Black Mountain,
North Carolina, I listen to what
sounds like Doris Day shooting
heroin inside Sly Stone's throat.

One would think that she fights
to get out, but she wants to stay
free in this skin. "Fresh,"
The Family Stone's album,

came out in 73, but I didn't make sense
of it till 76, sixth grade for me,
the Bicentennial, I got my first kiss that year,
I beat up the class bully; I was the man.

But for now, in my head, it's only 73
and I'm a little boy again, listening
to Sly and his Family covering Doris' hit,
driving down I-40;

a cop pulls me over to ask why
I'm here, in his town, with my Yankee tags.
I let him ask a series of questions
about what kind of work I do,

what brings me to town—you know
the kind of questions that tell you
this has nothing to do with driving a car.
My hands want to ball into fists.

but, instead, I tell myself to write a letter
to the Chief of Police, to give him something
to laugh at over his morning paper,
as I try to recall the light in Doris Day's version

of "Que Sera Sera"—without the wail

troubling the notes in the duet
of Sly and Cynthia's voices.
Hemingway meant to define
courage by the nonchalance you exude
while taking cover within your flesh,
even at the risk of losing
what some would call a melody;

I call it the sound of home.
Like when a song gets so far out
on a solo you almost don't recognize it,
but then you get back to the hook, you suddenly

recognize the tune and before you know it,
you're putting your hands together; you're on your feet—
because you recognize a sound, like a light,
leading you back home to a color:

rust. You must remember
rust—not too red, not too orange—not fire or overnight
change, but a simmering-summer
change in which children play till they tire

and grown folks sit till they grow edgy
or neighborhood dogs bite those not from your neighborhood
and someone with some sense says Down, Boy,
or you hope someone has some sense

who's outside or who owns the dog and then the sky
turns rust and the street lights buzz on
and someone's mother, must be yours, says
You see those street lights on don't you,

and then everybody else's mother comes out and says
the same thing and the sky is rust so you know
you got about ten minutes before she comes back out
and embarrasses you in front of your friends;

Home is Where

ten minutes to get home before you eat and watch some
of the *Flip Wilson Show* or *Sanford and Son* and it's time for bed.
And it's rust you need to remember
when the cop asks, What kind of work you do?

It's rust you need to remember: the smell
of summer rain on the sidewalk
and the patina on wrought-iron railings on your front porch
with rust patches on them, and the smell

of fresh mowed grass and gasoline and sweat
of your childhood, until he swaggers back to his car,
when the color of the day and the face
behind sunglasses and the hands on his hips

come back gun-metal gray
for the rest of this rusty afternoon.
So you roll up the window
and turn the music back on,

and try to remember the rust caught in Sly's throat—
when the song came out in 73,
although I didn't get it till 76,
sixth grade for me, the Bicentennial;

I got my first kiss that year,
I beat up the class bully; I was the man.

Within Our Gates
(Oscar Micheaux, 1919)

Theater doors open onto future
Scenes, while holding the option to return
Me to the past, as I watch a silent

Film few of my friends have seen. How moments
Like this do suspend time...The back of her
Neck when she lifts her hair... gone. I focus

On the film, but flashbacks hold disbelief
Hostage. Life now wills more life as a few
Scenes project on a white wall. What taboo–

Other than the near rape to which I bear
Witness, or maybe this lie I watch a
Man mouthing on screen to the white lynch mob—

Have I committed? Well, here's the spoiler
Alert: The girl on screen thought her lover
Would marry her—abandoned at birth by

Father, then by her fiancé–but now
She's pinned against a wall, and this white man
Thinks he's going to take what he thinks he owns,

When he discovers, once her clothes are ripped,
A birthmark: His illegitimate brand
On her chest. Years before, he took by force

The mother but cannot, years later, take
His own daughter. We call it a Lubitsch
Touch, now. But this was before we had a

Phrase for suggesting more in action than
We say in words. I can't fill the role of
All villains, only the ones I've lived; but

Home is Where

Victims I've played aplenty. And even
Threats of rape can change a man, a subtle
Violence to which a woman would not

Be made privy like when I've loved a woman
And then left her, left her before finding
The words to say goodbye.

TRAIN IN MY BRAIN

I love the sound of a distant train
I hear it travl'n in the fog and in the rain
Its whistle has its own personality
It's loud. It's soft, its moans and it screams
Its frequency somehow bends in the wind...
like smoke in a breeze

It can move from a point of presence and
Hurl me back to a time when I was enslaved
Pick'n cotton from sun up to sundown

Forty lashes for being proud
Forty and one, if I had a sharp tongue
Forty and two causin me and you would
sneak to read in the flickering flame
Forty and three for reject'n massa's name

Train tracks... contract... engines roar....
vibrating earth and a freedom door
Break for it. Freedom! Returning,
never more!... never more!... never more!... never more!

Today when I hear the sound of a moving train
I become empowered, it's hard to explain
When I hear that sound of a distant train
The memory is genetic, it's etched in my brain

Train in my brain. Freedom's door
Break for it. Freedom!
Returning... never more!... never more!... never more!...never more!
All Aboooard!

SHE BEGINS AGAIN

Pat her gently summer rain
She's uprooted and aflame
Woman alive...alive!

She times the seize, placid breeze upon her face
Transplants herself and blooms
Oh what a morning pure delight
Woman alive and free.

Slowly moving towards her prey
Past the tunnel bridge and dome, goes home
Fear disabled not deceived
She's not fragile, though bleeds

Watch her marvel ascend at will.
Stainless steel diamond spine
She begins again

IN SEARCH OF HUGO'S FURY

Hurricane Hugo

i am a starless night
in search of Hugo's fury

there is no peace in knowing
where the hurricane is headed

south of here

off the coast of charleston
down home cooking
okra soup gumbo and red rice
holler through my grandmother's kitchen
window

buttermilk biscuits storm the kitchen
and demand to be eaten
bellies fill themselves with fear
instead

the wind begins his ritual dance
of death and destruction
hurling his body through the air
swinging his arms to and fro
stomping ferocioulsy every tree
in his path

black eyed susans wrap themselves
tighter around their mother's earth

magnolias pray for their very own life
as i imagine terror releasing herself

rampaging through butterbean fields
collards and turnip greens

Home is Where

i imagine my people
every single one of them
huddled somewhere in prayer

as terror roams from house to house
stopping first at Aunt Eartha Lee's
the door is locked

Aunt Eartha Lee is too busy
cradling the home that has been
in her family 900 full moons
some 70 odd years or so

"You ain't got nothing to worry about
you hear, you come from a long line of
strong pine trees, papa built you to endure
this ain't the first hurricane you been
through and probably won't be the last"

the house seemed to sigh in relief
sticking out his chest he dared
Hugo to lay a hand on him

while Aunt Eartha Lee collected
what memories she could find
and stuffed them in a little suitcase
fore she lived too close to
the place where fish dream
off the shores of James Island

GOLDEN SEASON

shoulder my son over dead stalks,
feel him up there rocking,
a captain taller than we'll ever be alone

he trips cornrows like a one-man kindergarten,
scattering south toward woods senile in far haze,
yelping like a harmonica in search of a bootdance

if I could teach him I would tell him:
men are longitude, women latitude,
but wherever you stand is the top of the world

what else can you tell a boy who likes flying,
sparrows, tumbling and being amazed?
you know he's not a herd of palominos, but he thinks he's free

WE ARE GOING HOME

Some of us know all the cold seasons
some of us just got here
you can tell by the way they run out the house
bowlegged, buck naked, going, going, gone
they insist they're going somewhere

we are going home
we are sailing, sailing, sailing home

I saw the first cold season
cocktail bust the window, fire on the floor
mama and daughters scrambling for cover
papa and sons scrambling for water
outside, outrage:
twisted faces, screams, yelling
'go home, go home, go home...'

they were talking about the good thief
who checks the exits before he checks the jewels
good thieves, bad thieves
we are going home
leave everything on the edge: kingdoms lost
tongues cut, whips, whip scars, everything
you can carry on your back drop
right there dead on the edge

we are going home
we are all going home
we are sailing sailing sailing home

THE KILLING OF CARTER PEAMON

Mr. Hugh MacRae, of the Secret 25, the Ku Klux Klan,
and a decorated veteran officer of the Confederacy,
having been informed that a mass of rowdy negroes
were at the Sprunt Compress, sent a delegation
to determine if it was true that they were arming
themselves. He sent Mr. Heiskel Gouvenier,
a copperhead who had settled in Wilmington,
and a squad of sober Red Shirts with repeating rifles,
and the 70 year old negro Carter Peamon
was pressed into service to lead them there.
The negroes at Ninth and Nixon Streets
took the white men hostage, and intended to give
some return for the terror that they had witnessed.
Carter Peamon came to the defense of the white men,
and after several hours arguing for their lives
obtained their freedom and escorted them back
to the safety of Mr. MacRae. When they learned
of the threat the white men received the drunken
Red Shirts wanted to hang the negro until Mr. MacRae
insisted that would be wrong, but they should banish
him from their fair city. So the negro Carter Peamon
was taken to the depot and was on his way to exile when,
it was said, he jumped from the moving train, and
subsequently was shot dead by an unknown white man.

THE GAUNTLET

Daniel Wright, a negro politician and leader,
a distributor of colored dignity, was implicated
in the wounding of Mr. William Mayo who was
shot through both lungs in the cross-fire directed
on the coloreds running down Harnett Street,
even though there was no reliable testimony
that the negro Daniel Wright had been there.
The Red Shirt mob demanding surrender shot
into his freshly painted house. It was then
that the negro returned fire, killing Mr. Will Terry and
Mr. George Bland before the Red Shirts captured him.
The negro was hit in the head with a length of pipe
and made to run the gauntlet. Before he ran
fifteen steps he was riddled with bullets
and laid there in the street for most of two hours
before the Red Shirts allowed some of the coloreds
from the church to remove him to the hospital
where he was denied treatment,
and lingered for a day before he died.

BEFORE THE NIGHT IS DONE

Word came that the colored men from Navassa,
the small village west of the city, had rallied
and were coming to aid the coloreds in Wilmington,
taking a route that would have them crossing
the Hilton Park Bridge. The machine gun squad
rushed there to cut them off. The coloreds did not show,
so if they came into town they'd chosen another road.
At dark, small groups of negroes had gun battles
with the Red Shirt patrols that rode through Brooklyn,
firing volleys with shotguns, hunting rifles, and pistols
and leaving before the machine gun could get there.
The resistance of the coloreds was as big a surprise
as their successful tactics. Then the Red Shirts, armed
with Winchesters, walked the neighborhood
block by block, shooting at every negro caught outside
and searching every negro found at home.
The possibility of their own deaths a rising moon
riding every red shoulder. There was a report
from two undercover negro Pinkertons
that the coloreds were at a negro church
distributing weapons and organizing their defense.
The colored leaders were identified as Josh Halsey,
Tom Miller, and Josh Green, and it was clear
that one of them said, "Before this night is done
I will wash my hands in the blood of a white man."

SUNDAY VISIT TO A CAROLINA CHAIN GANG

Nobody works on Sunday, we were a Christian nation,
we kept the Lord's day sacred, even here.

The men lay around, most chained to a low standing
bar that ran the length of the camp. Others sought shade
where they could find it, within

the watchful eye of the white man with a comfortable belly
and a double-barreled shotgun. Two bloodhounds slept
under a small tree on his right..

I played marbles with myself while my stepfather talked
with one of his buddies, to whom he'd brought some chicken,
rice and a slice of pound cake Mama made.

"Don't run off now," he shot over his
shoulder, as I chased my favorite taw
down a slight incline.

Heard a man comin', comin' soon," his buddy said.
"Take most of these, I don't know where,
Georgia, 'labama, down that way.

Hear they got .steel mills, factories an' like that.
Anybody got no job got to go. Had a job last week,
don't count. Got to have a white man say you
workin for him now, right now."

I spotted a boy not much older than I, lying
At the edge of shade as the sun moved,
he had stretched as far as his chains allowed.

I started over to him to see if he could play.
"Get back there!" the white man shouted,
the camp aroused, men stood, rattled their chains
the dogs alert, stiffened. My stepfather ran to me,

pulled me back to where we'd been.

"You better go, man. You know how
things get when Charlie revved up".

"Can't take you no place." My
Stepfather chided, as he half dragged
me after him.

* After Emancipation former slaves were arrested on a myriad of
petty charges and held on impossibly high bail until some white
farmer or plant owner paid their fines and bound them into peonage,
perpetual debt.

A TRUE LIKENESS

To Richard Samuel Roberts 1880-1936
 "Son, you sure wore out; you didn't rust out."
 —Said by his mother on viewing his body.

Son, you sure wore out,
Son, you did not rust out.
You worked one job for bread,
You worked the other for love.

Son, you did not rust out,
No matter what the world will say,
You worked one job for love,
The plates you left will show them that.

No matter what the world will say,
The pics you left will show them that.
Those sacks of mail you hauled all day
Put bread on table for your brood.

The pics you left will show them that,
Those sacks of mail you hauled
Put bread on table for your brood.
At night your flash bulbs gave you life.

Those sacks of mail you hauled all day
Put bread on table, bought you film,
At night your flash bulbs gave you life
And life to those you made an image..

Put bread on table, bought your film,
Put gas in car to travel far,
Gave dignity to those you shot.
Son, you built a mighty house

Of photos that we love today.
You worked two jobs both day and night.
Son, you were just wore out,
You did not rust out, no you did not.
                    Adm, June 20, 2009

PLANES OF VIEW

A

I built my house where I shouldn'ta
'Cause I couldn'ta built it nowhere else.
Now the flood done come and took it,
like they knew it would.

When they picked us up off of the roof,
me and my parrot, they made me leave
him behind.

Boat ain't no place, them people say,
For no squawkin' bird.

Henry was some *good* company,
the best I had.

B

We sent out two plane loads
to San Diego and San Francisco,
twin giant hollow birds jammed with
our dogs and cats. This while
bodies floated like bundles
bounding gently in the toxic gumbo,
and that one over in Algiers* lay
soaking up sun and fetid air.

I helicoptered over the shifting scene.

These were folks I had seen
sitting on stoops, groups idling at corners,
never amounted to much. Oh,
those little ones, childr—

We even got out one parrot.
Ungrateful bird. Here we were
rescuing him, and all he could crack
was, "Goddamn your souls to hell!"

*District of New Orleans only slightly affected by flooding.

BACK THROUGH THE STORM DOOR

I left the South broken, a busted wing
and a crooked eye. Still, I wake mornings
with the taste of honeysuckle on my tongue.

The phone rings; voices weary with traveling;
wires weighed down with crows and thick heat.
I know it's the South calling me to christen
the born or bury the dead—
Lord, I'm still addicted to its touch:

He doesn't have long. If you're
going to come, it better be soon.

In bed hours later, my mind still
taloned to the phone's bad news.

Weed, codeine, scotch. I've ingested enough
fog and brain-ash to black out the moon.
But the crucible of the past is relentless,
grinding behind eyelids. Memories spark
wild along the nerves' telegraph. The lens
focuses backwards and the mind grays decades.

I dream my past a fragmented play, spliced
together with rawhide ties and silk thread.
It grows claws and jumps the stage: a beast
my hands don't know how to tame.

There is no balm for the past's dull ache.
When the blue jay rolls up his song,
the whole damn world spins down on me.
Falling back through the door,
I'm broken again.

SOUTHERN BOY'S JAZZ-HEAD BLUES

"Aspect of Negro Life #62 Song of the Towers" by Aaron Douglas

I. Growing Wings

It's guttural, this instinct hatched from marrow,
insisting I turn prodigal: be Be-Bop bound,
catch the Trane clattering up my spine.

Listen: they had to name Jazz before they
could pull Armstrong's tongue through his horn,
stamp it to vinyl. I itch for my turn.

Father sent tractors and oak-root to hammer
my feet to soil. I sent Sonny & Holiday
to kiss at the gates, gum the hinges.

Cursing birthright and family, I dialed up
Song of the Towers: Harlem's taboo of euphony,
Steel, and God-crazed sweetness.

In a month, I'm cutting heads with razor
blades and mirrors, staking my muses.
Soon, cravings outmuscled dreams.

I hock my axe for work gloves and a hardhat.
Winter careens me into hunger and shakes;
my body hollowed out, filled with a crazed hum.
            Everything I know is hunger or regret.

II. The Homecoming

I dream of sweetgrass and grunting tractors,
how the Delta lingers, unscratchable.

Momma still dreams an oak anchors my spine.
She can't see there's rot hollowing the flesh.

Memories clutched too tight twist to kudzu
and crabgrass. Creek water stills, turns stagnant.

Miles of barbed wire rust against my skin;
jittery eyes squint against the sun's glare.

It's Momma's fault I've come home. Not seeing
the horror I've become, she'll let me in.

> Li'l bro, you come home scratching track scars,
> jagged symbols; even a blind man can
>
> trace your history. I hear the Lime House
> refuses more of the ghosts you carry.
>
> So you store them, bundled up with box twine,
> a dry tinder to spark the grief you spread.
>
> Looks like you still slave to the hate of us.
> This farm, scorched and cratered, remembers you;
>
> I prophesized your return from shadows
> on the fields; curses darkening the sky.

Home is Where

My son, I wish your back unbroken from
the weight in your eyes, body a question

mark of sorrow, hostage to past laments.
I wish black sheep could be free of mythos.

I wish your fingers clean of tangled knots,
the one heirloom you didn't steal from me.

I forgive the moon for lighting your path,
the Good Lord for not troubling your compass,

the train's whistle for trumpeting you back,
even the street-signs for pointing you home.

PULL

I am told it was moonlight that ripened
your failing heart until it finally
cracked, sent the clockhands spinning

off your flesh. I was a coward, still 3,000
miles away, convincing myself that if I
came at all, I could never catch the dying hour.

Forgive me, brother. For decades, your
name has stretched my tongue to breaking.
But love and pain often anguish logic

Long ago, on a night like this,
I watched uncle rocket a coyote
skyward with a fistful of buckshot.

It slammed to the ground twisted,
skidding across the grass. Somehow,
it didn't know it was dead.

Front legs pawed the air as if leveled
by nothing more than errant moonlight.
Chicken feathers lined its muzzle.

It mewled, eyes tunneling through me
to the underbrush where its mate stood,
crosshaired down uncles' barrel

and already dead by every book and clock.
It stood, mesmerized no knowing, in this
world, every fool carries a twin heart.

Bang! I shouted and the underbrush
went wild with the mate's running. Still,
if animals have souls, two died that night.

Home is Where

Uncle cursed me under a killing sky.
Why, Boy? You know she'll hit
the coop later. Don'tcha know that?

This is my understanding
of the fear and silence
of these wounded nights:

the moon snares in the sweet
spot of the throat. Everything
that lives on is trapped in love.

ON MY 47TH BIRTHDAY

I watch the Grammy Awards,
the forty-seventh annual:

Alicia Keys, in white sleeveless top
and wrap-skirt, sings

as an orchestra plays
to her finger-zapping piano tune.

"If I ain't got you, Baby"
surges like a river.

Then she and Jamie Fox
duet, dance melodies:

"Georgia On My Mind."
Ray Charles nods.

How winter-calm the night turns.
I swivel on my black chair

now and again,
from the television's blare,

long after chocolate cake,
and butter pecan ice cream

while voices in sync
blend to greatness

until the weight of years carry me
back to my rooted home

lifting me away
where night hums its own song.

February 13, 2005

Home is Where

INTERROGATION OF HARRIET TUBMAN

You say I should escape with you,
follow the North Star that spills light
like my good breast drips milk.
I've already had my children snatched
from me as if they were brown eggs
in some nest. So you think I'm going
to trust you? What I'm going to eat?
An oak leaf? A pine needle? A twig?
My feet feel like axed wood.
My body feels like a sack of sweet potatoes.
You brave woman going to poke
that pistol in my side, make me walk.
I don't know what massa might think.
He said I was real good. And you say
you're taking me to freedom
that's as wide as this pitch black night.
Can you tell me what's waiting for us
in the thicket? Will a horseman be there
with his long black whip? A gun slung
over his shoulder to take us back
to that plantation? So why should I
follow you and the North Star tonight?
I hear a growl to our right.
I hear a yowl to the left.
You say keep walking with my feet
straight ahead, quick and quiet.
I think about my three children
snatched and sold. I want them back.
Will I ever see them again?
I push back branches, duck limbs
and side-step weeds. No water here.
Can your pistol shoot the horseman
off his horse without missing him?
I think I'll forget that my feet ache,
my hands sweat with each dark mile.
Sure we won't see coffles again?
Sure we won't witness whips again?
Sure we won't hear auction voices again?

AT THE TRAIN STOP

I imagine the quick hand:
Thelonious Monk waves
at red, orange, yellow leaves
from Raleigh to Rocky Mount.
Alone in this seat,
I peer out the half-window
at the rainbow of faces
bent toward this train
that runs to the irresistible Apple.
My determination to imagine Monk
glows like Carolina sun
in cloudless blue sky.
I try so hard to picture him
until his specter hunkers
at the ghost piano, foxfire
on concrete platform.
Now I can hear the tune "Misterioso"
float on sunlit air.
If notes were visible,
perhaps they would drift crimson,
shimmer like autumn leaves.
A haunting hunch shudders
into evening, a wordless flight.

THE CORE OF THINGS

She had this thing with fruit.
Rather, the seeds. An apple's seeds were small,
hard like the secret inner folds of the outer ear.
The pit of a peach looked much like her vulva.
The core of plums
the shape of her eyes.

She found herself looking at the core of things
about the time that the old persimmon tree
on the west end of the house
began to lean over at the burden of too-ripe fruit,
the oldest of the branches touching the ground.
Large persimmons, so large they had a history.
Rose-orange flesh that hinted at
perfection.

He said he was growing
weary of persimmons, had a pulsating
hunger for tangerines.

When the crow came searching for worms
she felt the sharp pain that consuming brings.
At her own core she wondered when the readiness
was truly all.

SINGING LESSON #2

In the dressing room, the three woman
Bind my breasts up tight, whisper in
amused Japanese that my breasts are stubborn and just
too big, even for a man to handle.
I am their baby.
They swaddle me in thin layers of cotton,
as I stand in my panties and bra in the chilly
backstage room.
They are a gathering of yellow,
chattering away at my navel
reaching up to dress their gaijin queen.
One old woman's hands systematically
pats my stomach with a cool wrinkled hand, then laces
pats. Laces, pats.
A final pat and she is done.
Looking down, my arms outstretched
as if I am on the cross,
I meet her smile and thank her with a confident: *onegaishimasu.*
Out of the thin wooden box resting on the floor comes the beautiful
Silken kimono, peacock green with a black obi.
They coo like doves about
how nice the color
looks against my dark skin,
begin to circle around me as they tighten, tighten the
thick belt to keep me tightly cocooned
in the kimono
as if pulling the lyrics out of my belly
onto my tongue.

Home is Where

AUNT VAUGHN'S MAP

The funeral was in 1996.
I didn't go. I didn't believe
you were dead. Not in the way they said.
Why be sad or angry or even numb? You are still
here. Be happy for me; I am not foolish.
I waited for you in the living room
by the expensive new harp you bought
before you passed on. I named her
Nzhinga since she was sitting there regal and ignored.
I took off my shoes at the door
the way you instructed everyone they must
do before stepping onto the snow white carpet
of your townhouse decorated like in a magazine
and while everyone went
to the funeral, I waited.
Here it is 2004, what I remember most
Is how you always
always did what you wanted.
Never apologized for
making the hour drive into the City for that
exquisite bread with the French cheese.
Never missed your biannual
trip to Aruba and the Maldives for anyone.
You were badaaaaaaaas.
You can rest now. You can finally make
good on the fancy mausoleum you
purchased and make yourself at home.
I found the map
you left me.
I am marking off new places,
the places you would have gone
places we might have traveled to together.
I am putting on the hat you left,
the one you had tucked away in the box marked:
"Exploration is at the heart of every *happy* black woman"

THE OFFICE

> She found the ledger
> at long last. The bitter
> proof, the open secret
> of her past. Little
> did she know, the dawn
> would match the dusk.
> She had all the names
> and figures, but nothing
> added up.

THE OFFICE

Elements: a checkbook register; at least four pens; a desk with drawers; gum erasers; coins; paper (at least nineteen sheets); dollars

1. Make a list of all your ancestors in a checkbook register.
2. Empty a desk drawer. Fill it to the brim with gum erasers.
3. Empty a desk drawer. Fill it to the brim with coins.
4. Make a lampshade of dollars.
5. Draft a design for a time machine. Build it.
6. Plan a successful slave revolt. Travel back in time to seven days before the emancipation proclamation (December 25, 1862) and carry it out.
7. Stand in a diamond shaped pattern, with each performer holding four sheets of paper and a pen. Estimate each performer's worth with a dollar amount on a separate sheet of paper. Don't account for inflation.
8. Make a list of everything you have in your possession that doesn't belong to you. Destroy the list.
9. Make a list of everything that belongs to you that is in someone else's possession. Attempt to get it back.
10. Hold coins in your hands until they sweat. Rub the sweat onto your bare arms. Repeat until you reek of money.

THE DINING ROOM

The chandelier is keeping
its many brilliant eyes on you.
Dangling above, it watches
you kiss the glass lips
of its cousin. But your head
is in the wine, in what your flute
contains, what can be tried
and consumed in one sitting.
Or maybe you are lost
in some wet, bitter notes
you imbibed long ago.
Either way, you don't stare
in awe at the prisms above,
or the old oak cabinet across
from your seat. You don't marvel
at the sturdy grace of the table,
where you rest your glass
or your napkin or fork,
not to mention the hands
that placed them there.

THE DINING ROOM

Elements: forks; knives; plates; dining room chairs; a tablecloth; a blindfold; a meal; a candle; an audio recording device; a playback device for the audio recording; water; a table; at least one carnivore

1. Using forks, knives, and plates, spell out your surname on a table.
2. Build a small house out of dining room chairs and a tablecloth.
3. <u>Performer 1</u>: Set a table. <u>Performer 2</u>: Sit at the table and blindfold yourself. <u>Performer 1</u>: Serve Performer 2 a meal. <u>Performer 2</u>: Eat the meal.
4. Light a candle. Set it on a table. Watch it burn until it burns out.
5. Eat dinner in silence.
6. Eat dinner; talk as you eat and swear never to repeat what you've heard.
7. Eat dinner; talk as you eat and record your conversation.
8. Eat dinner. Listen to a recording of a dinner conversation among strangers.
9. Write a letter to your ancestors. Use the underside of a table as your hard surface.
10. Eat a plate of dark meat.

THE COWS OF MT. SAN ANGELO

Groomed as royal, the cows of Mt. San Angelo
have the abundant pastures of the mountain
to themselves; evergreen grass all year round.
Plump and healthy, no cows can be bigger
than these multiethnic crop of Virginia cows.
Black, brown and white-faced like a mask,
they mow the grass gracefully; no hostile figures
or irritants to worry about. Young ones
prance to their mothers when I come close,
but there's no fear of poachers in this pasture.

The cows of Mt. San Angelo cannot cover
the entire meadow that's green with abundance.
They know not that outside famine kills a number
and rinderpest and poachers are on the loose.
They are half-covered in lush grass without bother
of ticks—above, birds sing their hearts away
in the paradise they share. There's no Fulani
herdsman lashing at them to take the right course
in the lines they always fall into in the open space.
They yawn at night from the day's plentiful food.

They have the garden world to themselves—
they know not the harsh struggle or sweat
that each day brings; they are self-assured.
They share the road and their shit bothers none.
If one should be a cow, wouldn't one wish to be
one of the selected cows grazing Mt. San Angelo?
But, after all the pleasures, will the butcher
spare them the fate of other cows envious of them?
The cows of Mt. San Angelo belong to a class
of their own—treated royally for the king's table.

SAY CAROLINA

for My Palmetto State
after Rita Dove

Nothin finer than a tea drunk gurl
raised on peaches   sugah   honey chile & y'all
Nothin finer than her palmetto & crescent moonshine
pinched and dangling on each ear
Nothin finer than her sass
her sweet potato thick waist
spreading from Low Country to Upstate
bible belt cinched and clinched
sportin 47 patches that work
a rice cotton & tobacco shimmy
from sun up to sundown

Carolina's hot
& cotton's supposed to let you breathe
but under her honeysuckle & jasmine print skirt
all you feel is the burn of 9000 ebony fires
& Denmark Vesey leading the charge
whispering in quilt-stitch code
for a stolen people to rise up
sharpen their dreams
and fly

Carolina's a gumbo
sweet grass grace mixed with old money
Look down her cobblestone roads
laced with Spanish moss you feel the worlds
between the worlds   Rainbow row colors
blending with auction block songs   Part the veils
but don't get too close to her port waters
even if you know how to swim cause

Carolina's deep
She's a complicated Lady
look beyond the magnolias and mint juleps
she all plantation upfront & Middle Passage baggage behind
She's had a hard time carrying the weight
but Carolina don't care cause she the bomb
all muskets & canons when she lifts her skirt
Shoot Carolina will blow your mind
with the twisted & strange fruit
she both bears & wears
Say it again Carolina don't care
She done acquired the taste,
you can tell how she walk & talk
she likes how it hangs

Home is Where

AUTHORS' CONFERENCE

At Alexander Elementary School

Greenville is my home,
always calling me back

to flow around bends
and back roads.

Calls to me to open
my Palmetto mouth

pour like an ebony waterfall
—extend verse like a familiar song,

Asks me to stir young minds,
that cause black kids to rise,

talk back like they were taught
on church pew Sunday mornings.

In the gym this music catches
the air while mamas and grandpas

dance overhead like Sandburg's Fog.
The circle set, all the children ride

across Carolina on my wings
of *If I Ain't African If I Ain't African.*

As the moment *moves on.*
The principal calls me over,

introduces me to a dark-skinned boy,
Jamar: wide-eyed and awake.

He shakes my hand.
Pipes up unplanned,

You don't look like no author.
What does an author look like?

You know how he looks,
when he be looking in that book.

Jamar read the same books
I read 3 decades ago

his ungrammatical tug
takes my five year-old hand

to daffodils & nightingales
that unfold and sing, but not to me.

Lonely & haunted
blank   quiet   stares—

no gospel or jazz thrum,
no cowrie, crow or drum,

I come back
for Jamar's ebony eyes

looking at me,
looking like I look.

Home is Where

CLOSE AS I GET TO CURSING

Where I come from, hate seethes
like a fresh brew on the tongue everyday

Why add to the pot? Bile leaves
an unpleasant aftertaste.

Why lend words to curse the earth?
Aren't our skies full enough of soil-weep

and southern tree-lean? Gut rot grows
in the bowels. I say shit it out.

If ever I hurled a stone it was in my mind.
Damning the damned ain't worth the spit.

ANATOMY OF A BOX

I waited patiently for the Lord
                                 Psalm 40:1

A gimlet is a drink with gin
not the tool that makes holes to breathe,
but it did while you rode first upside down,
then on your side, and so many other directions,
smelling cotton you were trained to pick up
and put into a sack
as soon as you could walk far enough.
You were rested on,
expounded upon, almost
left behind with eyes swelling,
the *cold sweat* of death,
nonetheless delivered
to William H. Johnson, Arch Street,
Philadelphia.

MAMA TRIED

My son wants to put bad guys in jail.
He is a superhero, the only superhero in town,
and that's what superheroes do,
Green Lantern, Captain America, Superman . . .
And that's what you do to bad people.

This is what he tells me
on the way home from church on
Wednesday night. I should agree with him, but it's too hard
after divorce class when I'm feeling guilty
for asking his daddy to leave and breaking my covenant.

I say *you know mama's been to jail.*

AN INAUGURATION OF HOPE

I feel the energy of those long gone
they're coming back now for one last look
to see a native son with African roots
that run deep through Kenyan soil
with blended blood from European
and Cherokee love pumping through his veins
put his hand upon a Bible of another great man
who helped free those shackled and chained
mentally physically contained within fields
picking grains and cotton under the hot broiling sun
while being overseen with a whip and tar
the tide is turning toward a trail to change
where tears helped mat down dust that rose
with hatred by those who rode through the night
wearing white but carrying hate dark and deep
the energy is pushing away the years past
opening up for future possibility of chants
yes we can, yes we did, and yes we will do
we will do what is needed to ensure that generations
to come will be blended into one nation indivisible
under God no matter what the atheist say
we will work to lift up this man with his hand
on a Bible taking on the challenges of today
and tomorrow we will show him honor with respect
always remembering that ancestors are watching
they are nodding approval because maybe now
deep festering wounds can begin to heal.

THE SCRAPBOOK

Finch

The first picture I turn to is of Junnie Finch. I reminisce
in the room where I sit like a kid nostalgic as the old
snapshots, this one taken weeks before Finch was shot to
death while breaking into a man's house. In it, he's only fifteen.
His brother handed me this photo after the funeral;
and bent over one end of the desk, I'm trying to remember
his thin face bulging with joy as he runs down a field.
His eyes are wide without a blink, guiding a football into his
dark and sticky fingers. I still see the quarterback's toss, the pig
skin spinning through the air, and Finch, as if he was headed
to the Hall Of Fame, leaves behind the slow legs of a defender
lost in the open field, a swirl of dust at his feet,
and with one hand, he snags the ball for a touchdown.

Swift

Across the page, there's a shot of my best friend Swift,
and the past comes off as the present in what happens to
be a day of cameras and smiles when he was crowned Kentucky's
high school tennis champ, with the trophy to prove it.
I think it was June among the crowds under the nightlights
at the court, the place that haunted him with *could've been* and *what if,*
after he grew tired of competition, deciding not to turn pro.
Later, he worked a few manpower jobs to see if he could
find a fit that inspired the same sense of self
he got from playing the game; but he changed jobs often,
like switching ends on the court, between points,
as if he wasn't meant to stay in one place too long.
For me, his loss was the worst. It was as though he didn't
see death coming when it caught him by surprise.
I heard he was killed by a roommate, a murder unleashed
by anger, over a little money, that his body was found
tied up and floating in the Mississippi between Minneapolis
and St.Paul. Yet, when I'm out at night, I feel him walking

with me like air from the last dark shower of raindrops,
as though he's letting me know, we're still close.

Ralph

Down the page, a slip of silver borders the edge,
and there's a black and white of my crooning buddy Ralph.
His picture carries the biggest smile in the scrapbook—
flashy as a star, intense like a flame. As kids, we sang together
in a band, and when we needed someone to hit the high notes,
he could turn his tenor into a canary singing its way out
of a cage. After I left the band to get back in school,
Ralph started gigging with other guys in dives and juke joints,
but drugs followed him from stage to stage. He never got far,
never made it big. I don't know how he held it together,
but he kept singing even through his own demons. The last time
I saw him, his front teeth had been knocked out.
He smiled at me with his dark gums, the damage there—
that picture, the loss inside his mouth, two years before his life ended
from an overdose, or sadness.

Snuffy

Next to Ralph's picture, one of my favorites, a Polaroid
of my childhood chum, Snuffy, smiling on stage in a college play,
where the audience sees a woman leave a man. Snuffy's a bartender
with a white cloth wiping spilled beer off the counter,
and consoling the man sagged in sadness.
Now gone from cancer, I remember what Snuffy told me
about art—*make it new, make it different, make it yours,*
choice words, picture words, this mirror of Snuffy
and others here in the squares. The resonance of his mantra
makes me smile, until the words fade, leaving a warmth
in the room, as though the sun in its silence,
its pure light had schooled the birds inside me to
the simple ways of memory so they can always fly.

SOJOURN

It Takes One To Know One.

Snuffy comes out of Miss Betty's house and ragamuffins rocking
rigs and barges of oil men on the Ohio.
Junnie Finch comes out of a backbone and field hand resistant to
slave-traders from *The Good Ship Jesus.*
A slave ship comes out of an asshole to relegate captives
contained by pirates with weapons pointed at the heart.
A shotgun comes out of Jim Crow bondage.
Crowing Jim comes out of Willie Lynch, the blaze of a cross burning,
white sheets grazing the ground where nightriders turn the grin
to blood and Neo Nazis read Mein Kampf, wear swastikas,
seek and find Skinheads where Lucifer fell off the crystal bridge
when he forgot to watch his step.
A grin comes out of jackanapes and g-men with wire taps
in the rain and hands carrying tape recorders—all the piss ants
in the world it takes to infest a home.
A home comes out of the brick on Von Spiegel Street in Southwick,
where kids in winter coats cover their heads with hoods, wear waterproof
gloves, curl their fingers around snowballs to throw at City Hall
and hope it melts like a snowman so they can see what goes on there
between those walls. They want to find a future. They don't want
the freezing snow. They already know the cold.
Ralph comes out of riding the bus from Southwick across town
through rain and sleet to his girlfriend's house at one in the morning.
A kiss comes out of a dream like a child holding hands
with a stranger while walking across a frozen lake.
Swift comes out of a tennis ball hit against the wall, winning
matches, smiling at how the trophy looks in the newspaper.
Snuffy comes out of a path to public housing, welfare, food stamps
in the pocket, a kid chewing bubblegum over his homework,
a blackout, a curfew after the riot, the first fire of protest
marches and meetings at a street corner, signs of enlightenment
where thugs and cops with loaded guns co-opt the scene like steam
heat warms a catacomb too small for privacy, big enough for seven
earthquakes, six tornadoes surviving the living and the dead.

Death comes out of being and the absence of being like the time
I got swooped up and turned back, stillborn, no heartbeat, no breath,
a bird dead inside an egg, no crack in the shell, no light coming in,
eyes shut, a soul stopped in its course, thrown into nothing
without having seen the sky on skin here.
A bird comes out of the heat of summer where the soul
ditty bops with the spirit near a basketball court, a pick-up game,
brown skin slick with sweat, hints of soap and aftershave,
breeze cutting between the cornrolls, voices immersed in the ear.
Listening comes out of silence.
Silence comes out of Ralph dying under the moon, in his pajamas,
in bed, in moan, in the final drop of music he heard
before he said goodbye.
The moon comes out of Southwick, salt of sweat,
salt of earth, a toothpick in the mouth, a funny face.
Snuffy comes out of a nap on the couch.
Junnie Finch comes out of a door hidden by trees
marked like algebra on a chalkboard.
Ralph comes out of the curtains on stage, a connoisseur of limelight.
The microphone in his hand comes out of a pawnshop.
Swift comes out of a window when his ride pulls up in front
of the house, and blows the horn for the last time.

Home is Where

FATHERLESS CHILD

some times i feel like a motherless child,
because i been fatherless
my whole life

I don't know how to treat a wife,
my relationship skills came
from pimps and womanizers

So hell yes I like treating
women like a pieces of meat
and glorifying sex,
that's the attitude that was given to me
by my elders

The Cosby Show was cool
but reality is a pain
and my reality was a three bed room house,
with one closet, and one bathroom,
with plenty of rats and roaches
in the poverty stricken South Dallas, TX

I had a loving but lost mother,
a mean grandmother,
a cousin
or two
or three,
and an uncle I was afraid of
because, he was obsessed with committing sin,
he loved fighting and going in and out of the pen,
and I was trying to escape this place
but I was only ten
and thinking,
maybe it would be different
if I had a father

he didn't have to be a doctor like Cliff Huxtable,
he just had to be there,
to teach me how to be a man,
teach me how to ride a bike,
teach me how to fight,
and explain to me why
I have these words in my head
and this incredible erg to write,

it's sad being from a bastard generation,
because men cum and go so much
not realizing the lives they destroy
because souls can't grow with out a certain touch
and there are so many black sons and daughters
that need to be messaged back to life

sometimes I feel like a motherless child,
cause I been fatherless my whole life time

not saying it because it rhymes
I'm saying it because it hurts,
kids are feeling worthless because
their shoes doesn't match their shirt
or because they don't have a gold grill,
that because we have a generation of baby makers
without leadership skills,
who are being raised by hip pop and pop culture
So
you aren't cool if you have a degree
but you are if you have a strike,
that's because men are striking out at being fathers
like Barry Bonds without steroids
and pops I'm trying to avoid being you,
because
I don't want my son or daughter writing a poem like this, I don't
want them living in a world like this,
and I don't want them feeling like this,
lost, empty, and un-whole

Home is Where

please God help us fatherless children

we are the roses growing from the concrete, begging for
water and light,

we are the lost children in Babylon wanting to be free

we are those kids sitting on the curb
watching every car that passes by,
wishing it was daddy coming home
lost, but found,
quiet, but loud,
happy, but sad,
you know us great pretenders, needing love

sometimes I feel like a motherless child,
cause I been fatherless my whole life

home is where

in my back pocket :: nailed up over
my bed :: buried in rules :: *sit up straight and*
mind your manners :: under my nails ::
i'm sure it's around here somewhere ::
going, going :: that one, the one where i went
to be borrowed and blue :: the one i left for
carolina :: oh i could suit a case of you :: i

can't put my hands on it at the moment :: have
you got a spare :: the one that made me
feel guilty :: for months the cat sucked
the fur off the tip of her tail :: the hour when
sunshine angled in each morning :: i

can't leave it without it :: in a couple tunes
you could listen to :: maple trees :: it was
just at my fingertips :: the kind of warm you can
feel :: the one that was well-seasoned ::
the one that was near the other one :: where
moonshine cast shadows :: the first one :: *don't say*

ain't :: *keep your dress tail down* :: the one where
it stayed cold all winter :: come june, wisteria
just pulled down the lattice, it was so thick ::
like that late spring night, the fireflies
a carpet over the field :: up the street from my
friend :: at the bottom of the hill :: one
of eighteen, and counting :: what's yours is
mine :: the one where i repacked some
to make room for someone :: it was a real
hit with all my visitors :: the one that spit
me out :: where the cat is :: i wouldn't know it
from a hole in the ground :: *don't ever get*
behind in your rent :: where we unpacked our

yes :: i danced in the living room :: i believe
i'm forgetting one :: puerto rican coffee ::
going, going :: the odd one that came
to a sharp point :: built-in bookshelves :: blue
carolina skies calling :: maybe i left it
in my bag :: down by the riverside :: over
my shoulder :: the first we chose with us in
mind :: where the organ is :: where the dust

one way to say it

wait for the leaves to show
                            their light and their dark
         sides : the wind will draw out
                                   their two truths : the sun

            will shine on both as if
they are the same and
                    in that way they will be :
       you must choose : to draw

               near hold a leaf still and
watch it grow its sap-
                  rich veins loud with life : or

          to stand back view the whole
     tree at once and clap
               as the wild herd of leaves
waves. do what you will
       do. they are your hands.

ballad of bertie county

i.

it was our hope to get there long before
dark, but this part of carolina had been
dark for two hundred years or more:
dim-lit by white flames of cotton on thin

brown stalks. we were answering a call,
braving klan country to bring black folks
city words with rural roots. we were all
smiles with rough edges, telling bitter jokes.

ii.

sistah's house must be pretty big, we
joked, half-expecting to be bedded down
on cots and couches after eating all the
collard greens we could. the last town,

as sleepy as we were, some twenty, thirty
miles behind us now. we were gunning
our mouths, didn't hear the whispers we
should have heard. time's savage cunning.

iii.

around us, the trees silhouetted, blackened,
and disappeared into vast carolina night.
we chased our headlights. our pace slackened
when we spotted red-brick columns and white

picket fence. a gravel driveway led through
the columns towards a noose of yellow light

above a shuttered door. ancient pines grew
on either side, rising thickly, quickly out of sight.

iv.

not knowing what we'd gotten into, we
got out of the car. the land seemed to sigh,
a cricketless silence. we still didn't foresee
the plump white woman who greeted us. *hi,*

you must be . . . come in. welcome. farewell,
welfare, we thought, and crossed the thresh-
hold. inside, one glance told us the deal. hell,
it really was a big house. memories in the flesh.

v.

no sign of mammy anywhere. no "wooly heads,"
no "pickaninnies," no grinning boy-men, in any
pictures, on any knick-knack shelves. our beds
in innocent, menacing rooms. how many, how many

slaved here? echoes of injuries rushing down
the spiral staircase at us, seeping from the wood
floor like sweat. none of us ever meant to drown
first-hand in such a flood. fate got us good.

vi.

burgundy candles burned, bleeding onto
the mahogany table. portraits of the mistress
and master, in silk and suit, hung like two
crimes on the opposite wall. our distress

Home is Where

crawled our skin like lice, as our hostess's aunt
and mother fished out story after story
from their wine glasses, dripping their debutante
drawls all over us, draping us in old glory.

vii.

we were never alone together, till she left
us for the night in our three unholy
rooms. gathering in one, we mourned the theft
of our choice, our right to claim, solely

for the sake of our historied hearts, *i NEVER.*
one of us drew a vial of oil from a pocket,
anointed our heads, hands, feet. *evil's clever.*
touch your windows and your door. and lock it.

viii.

there were forty-seven blacks enslaved here,
she'd told us. i sat up with all the lights
on till my eyelids dropped like tears. fear
dragged me through sleep, despite our rites.

i dreamed of forty-seven fiddles shrieking
dixie, forty-seven bales of cotton, forty-seven
hounds a-howling, forty-seven planters leaking
pus between brown thighs, and not one heaven.

ix.

morning. november's anemic sunlight swooned
across the yard and, beyond, the desolate field.
i sought sights to prove we weren't marooned
in 1850, 1940. watched an elder wearily wield

a rake, inherited work he'd spent a lifetime
doing, his payment a pittance little more than
slave wages. *historic preservation:* pastime
for mother and aunt, livelihood for this man.

x.

downstairs, in the kitchen, we sipped coffee,
waited on scrambled eggs. through a second
door, a room we hadn't seen last night. off we
went, drawing near the portrait that beckoned

us. *who's that?* we asked. *sis harriet, they
called her. harriet gatling. she was cook here, after
slavery.* so: *stand here,* said miss lady one day.
i want to paint you at . . . um . . . rest. laughter.

xi.

we breakfasted, packed, followed them
to the center to read our poems. exercise
equipment had been pushed to the gym
walls. *the only other place nearby of enough size*

for such a program is hope plantation, our hostess told
us. counting our blessings and our meager
but warm black audience, we let our words unfold
a map of farms and cities, migrations of the eager.

xii.

it was our hope to recover a newer world
before dark, but we had to drive across
centuries to get home. our directions wrong,
but our wills strong, we bore our mutual loss

Home is Where

in anything but silence, till we saw rocky mount
twinkling along the highway, a tight necklace
of lights. we swore to log this passage, to account
for this double-crossing, to etch an inerasable trace.

—for lenard and teresa

where's carolina?

east of childhood, north of
                    capitol offenses, just west
         of a big blue treasure chest :
                              wet coffin of neglected bones.
              in the veins, unnoticed as
a pulse. at a counter : sitting in
         varicolored eloquence. behind
                         the mystery of the magnet. home
              of horton, poetry's bondsman :
                    between anger and awe. below
the line, overrated, underestimated.
                    helms territory : within a belt,
         an expanding waste. atop hades :
                         persephone's threshold. beside
cloud-hooded mountains.
                    outside time : a coltrane solo.
                         far from fatal. after all.

CLAIM

My tongue, every atom of my blood, form'd from this soil, this air,
Born here of parents born here from parents the same, and their
parents the same...
                                                    —Walt Whitman

Sun reaching through the bus window makes her a flame.
White cloth twining her head ignites the tip of a body
Dressed all in white, as if readied for dipping in the Sunday stream,

Though she hardly knew the woman who would have counseled
Her preparation—reminding her not to fight the preacher, just
Lay back, meet the water with the ease of the unburdened—

Who had left these backwoods, dispossessed and angry,
By this same road but northward, like ancestors
Who traced rivers, moss, nocturnal light to the city.

This trip reverses that repudiation of the South.
As she recounts her grandmother's deathbed wishes,
Reviews her own bitter struggles, she's a torch

Glowering in midday. Old cruelties mark this soil.
Its memory takes trope in jolts her crippled back records,
And she winces, reminded of a new corporate toll.

But a disability settlement's reluctant reparation
Is just enough to purchase her inheritance,
Make her the family's agent fulfilling old ambition.

Gnarled braids escape her headwrap, signify on native trees
Warped by heavy fruit. The house those trees built—
Taproots drawing her forebears' blood and sweat, their cries,

And prayers into the very walls—will be her grandmother's again.
The Greyhound's bringing their twinned spirits home,
Where she'll make for them an unassailable shrine.

ON AGING

In the airport, I survey the middle-aged passersby and, finally,
count myself among them. I remember the famous photographer
years ago at the artist colony who photographed and interviewed me
and my new friend for her project on aging. A glorious prospect I thought,
dreaming of wisdom, old errors eroded, old hurts muted, cushioned
in the gathered skein of years. And your looks? she urged.
She didn't picture in mine those images of my ancestors—bronzed,
stalwart skins that didn't crack, heads held up by necks that refused to sag . . .
Only diminished muscles, the lessening of the body's readiness, its quick
response to my will, concerned me—though that would be some time off yet.
Older, she must have thought me a naïf at 33, but, faintly smiling,
snapped shots of me in motion: blurred defiance.

As they saunter or hurry past, the particulars of the in-betweeners—
the not-quite-elderly—are more poignant in the terminal's light:
A petite New England society hostess in butter sweater, the olive
green of her Italian loafers and designer tote a refinement,
a buffer. Her husband's salt-and-pepper hair still full.
Their casual counterparts—the whitebread, Wal-Mart, mainstream lot—juggle
overstuffed luggage and gifts, greet children and strollered grandkids in clumps.
Where are the poets, I wonder, whose wrestlings with words
have stamped them numinous survivors, inexpressibly kin.

And now they come on thicker, too many to study them all—the tattooed,
grey-haired hybrids, the slightly-tinged-at-the-temples suaves, the dour uprights,
the cloud-bearing, slack-jaweds, the permanently pregnant men
too numerous to believe . . . And, here and there, real beauty: the softened face a
vault of savored pleasures, serene sprawl of a mouth, flare of far-reaching,
   curious eyes. . . .

Home is Where

WAR STORIES, EARLY 21ST CENTURY

1. Pax Homelandia

Late afternoon in the residential precincts
of downtown Decatur, an alarm is ringing at the
Lock & Key—a situational irony.
Hundreds of brass keys, small bones
of a parent lodestone hung in placid rows.
But something has sprung their almost
ceremonial order and set the place to shrilling,
its jangling protest released
into a sluggish parade of sedans,
blades of unflinching grass, the blank
faces of neighbor shops. In Baghdad

women keening is the soul-alarm announcing
the unholy state of amputation, husbands
and children so many blasted shells
strewn in the streets, the fields . . . The widows
now have a permanent pact with pain,
a cracked mindscape the twenty-cents bottles
of Valium must plug, the pills too smooth
to hold, they keep falling out, and more
and more choked down, pushed through
to staunch the awful ringing in the ears.
The once-wives-and-mothers wear black,
wail and swoon as TV cameras eye them,
unblinking, mutely recording. But the pills,
plentiful and discrete, numb the shock, leave each
to her private closet in the avalanche.

Soon someone will come to quiet the loud cries
of the lock shop—the heedless employee
who had stepped out for coffee, or the owner
with the code to bring peace to this street again.
The air, faintly stirred, will resume its benign striations.
Elsewhere, a kingdom is appeased—
the catatonic calm deafening.

2. Way Out West

This time the women go into the desert,
past its parched earth and plants,
up to the ranch—emblem of a remnant frontier
where true cowboys once eked out
existence—there to its gate and drive
and sprawling buildings hidden from scrutiny,
to make their stand against the killing.

The resident cowboy has no flock to worry
over out in a meandering pasture—
where one once feared the poacher's raid
or Indian attack aimed to liberate the beasts
from what was also a reservation and basic
genocide, though no one is equipped to think
of cow genocide or forced horse servitude, you
see how absurd it sounds, and though the Indians
have been preemptively dealt with at this juncture—still,
his presence begs security. He looks out
over the wavering grounds, heat rising
to his mistrustful eyes, and spies them—
the small band of women, pitching camp,
come, as others had, for answers.

He has the hungry jaw and feral eye
of one who has patrolled the range of an inner
Ponderosa, not unlike its cinematic namesake,
yet a vaster homeland to infinite dangers:
the biological weaponry of snakebite and vengeful
cacti or indigenous enemy combatants who trespass
against the confines of reservations to war-dance
in his peripheral vision. If they could get past
the gate, the long drive, and the checkpoints beyond,
to the ranch house rooted like a hitch-post
in the high noon of his paranoia, the women
would ask the figurehead cowboy some hard
questions about truth, justice, compassion.

Home is Where

And what could he tell them—with ghost herds
and the dusts of the plains bearing down upon him
like shadows? When in his wild vigilance
had he ever recognized such things?

He had seen some of them before, these women,
maybe on CNN, late, their sound-bites unfriendly.
Unnatural out here, he thinks—like reality TV
actresses—and smiles at this cleverness and eases a bit.
Hadn't the aides said that they would go away soon?
The doctor had prescribed something to help,
but he hated the dark abyss right before losing
consciousness that reminded him of those first nights
in a lonely bedroom at the end of the hallway
separating him from his father. He checks
his face again in the SUV's side mirror. He wonders
if the press conference makeup will cover up
the telling signs of fatigue. God, if only
they would leave him alone, maybe he could
just stay here, hunt to his heart's content.

3. Killing Grounds

They won't tell us what happened. Or can't.
By design, it gets locked up in some space
made by something displaced—a calcified
liver or brain. A cell. A fitted box.

Stiffened versions of themselves—
refusal to bend
or shell-shocked rigor mortis of struggling heart.

Canvassed. Counted. Cornered.
Suited up and sent upriver. Downriver. Abroad.
Parceled out. Packaged. Damaged.
Expired. Returned. Reinscribed.

All those brash boys who ran their paces,
lapped the courts—both kinds—or the streets

in half-mast pants and multi-colored transport—
quasi-car-or-spaceship—encasing their feet.
Anxious men whose audacity took them through
vacant lots—glass shards on asphalt—to reassemble
as angels under hoops—the only halos they're allowed.

Always prisoners.
Lately—conveniently—
terrorists.

NERUDA, AT THE SEA

That familiar furrowed face,
its patina of late longing,
the sea, so calm
he feels nude in its presence—

Stark gauntness of his back,
flesh surrendered to reveal
hollows of shoulder blades,
knobs where wings might sprout—

Suppose him dying then—
yet the moment not robbed
of its sweetness, vastness, his
grasp of its elegiac form—

Swaying,
as into a lover's embrace.

MANIC

Like time, she finds empty corridors
  to slide into.
Seeking solace in laced fingers and bobbing head.
In silence, she hopes to finally unlock a door to sanity,
  tranquility.
Speaking in riddles, she's misunderstood.
She sits.
She waits praying, praying someone will hear her quiet screams
  and save her.
Save her before it's too late.

YOUR DAVID, MY SAUL

for Meka

I.

At sunset I watch the legions
train slowly through Zion,
loitering in our narrow streets
like brash perfume.
That armor is a bulwark of commotion
that covers over the cries of boys
straddling mothers' hips,
their thick arms stretched out
toward your indifference.

II.

When you call me closer
I always pretend
I did not hear you the first time.
You beckon again
and though I am afraid
I wonder what would happen
if you could hear my music clearer.
But I cannot trust you.
Your hand hangs wearily from the bed
too close to the spear
So I watch you as I approach,
And even though your eyes are closed
I slide the spear away
so that I am between it
and you.

TACT

Phil said
so what happened
and Sosh goes
Well, my BP

Blood Pressure

was up
it hasn't been up
the whole time
and they told me to come on in

it's
they call it preeclampsia
high blood pressure
it can be dangerous
so they said she needed to come now
they tried to turn her four times
'cause she was breech

That hurt like hell

basically
she was butt down
and you know
they just don't come out that way

Phil laughed

yeah   right

and I was thinking
how she sounded like a pro
how before
she might have said something snappy

Home is Where

like   well,
maybe whores' babies
come out that way
butt down
and I'm not a whore
you know, just as a joke
a little levity
amazing that she didn't even think
to say that

A FEW YEARS IN

For now,
I've brushed the leaves into a corner
to remember how the patio looks.
I open the screen door
to yell for approval.

On cold nights
the air smells scoured clean,
and even in the city
the sky darkens just enough
to see stars.
I point out the orange moon
and hold her like the male lead.
When I squeeze too tight
she never pushes back
like she needs room.

Sometimes I show love like
I don't want her to wonder
if there's anything more to know.
Every so often in the stillness,
More work comes down
around us.

DOLL

dey tooks me f'om out de fiel   wourk in de
kichin   scaird fo ta tak it   kill ya if ya don tak it
right   took'ded pennyroyal seeds 'n tansy root
knot ma innards sompin turbul   aint hurt haf so
much as wen he shunt huh in ma belly   ma marige
man 'ready gived me to   had to f'om de fielhans fo'
den   I gets mor'n birf pangs fo my trubles   a
ev'ra christmas gif fo'm de Massa   'n dey wuz
sol   all dem sol   didn wont no mor   didn wont
no mor suffrin   gon tak rue   or de cotton root
but be's so sikly   de midwife givd de strop a black
haw   so's I names yo mama Rue   fo huh ta
memba   I didn 'tend fo huh ta suffa no pain
black haw kep huh heah   onst de seed plant   seem
lik de root taked holt   Mama'nem name me
Doll   gues cuz I'se so lite
so's I names yo mama   Rue   fo ta gi'huh strenf

SILLY

de Mistess taked huh to huh own selfs   took'ded ma chile   ma Rue
fo' ta suckle   huh own chile wudn't root   shrivels up   dont wont
de nipple   didn had no funral   night buried n de gardn   Rue
pull hard   ease huh sum   huh bresses hard swoll wid de milk   de
Massa dont sleep de same room   I sleeps de pallet on de flo   Mist-
ess keep Rue in de bed   call huh Mar'gret Rose lik Rue huh own
dont call huh
by huh name   de Massa don't kno Rue not *huh* chile   she look'ded
so lik him   huh lite hair turnt red   'n dey birf chile wuz a gurl
hiz mine on de rumbul a de talk a war   den he ride off wid hiz
sord   Rue in huh purty dress   Mistess say *Mar'gret Rose stop*
pokin n de flowers n de gardn   Doll git huh away f'om dose ninnies
n de yahd   A white chile shoud'na play wid no niggahs   Bring huh
n de house fo she get muss

       I picks huh up   she 'gins ta cry   "Da" "Da"

       I wont ta slap huh silly

FICKLE

Mistess! Mistess! De fiels n stoop 'zerted.
Mose   Sella   Banjer'nem don gone.

Mistess no one ain't here cept Zarina'n me.
Shet yo stinkin mouf 'n scatter yo lazy behin

de Mistess say or *I'll leave ya to dem Yankees.*
Damn yo yellow hide. Dis war on account a you'n.

Dey'll split ya down da middle, brown
'n serve ya as a to-day roas'. Now move!

I duz. Firs I gits de horse de Massa lef
whut jus foal 'n hitch huh to de wagn,

climb de stair 'n fetches Rue 'n huh sleepin
blanket 'n gentles huh down in de wagn bed.

I runnin ta tell de Mistess we be ready
'n stop. Don' kno how far we kin gits but

I kno de Yankees whah de fi'ahs be
n onliest dis be meanin sompin n de worl ta me.

SEPIA PICTURE POSTCARD

"Look pretty for the postcards."
Children all smiling, the crowds.

The crowd smiling, children all
cheer, playing with souvenirs.

Cheers. Playing with souvenirs,
gentlemen pose with their catch.

Look pretty for the postcards.

Gentlemen pose with their catch,
gin-flask gripped, shared mouth to mouth.

Gin-flask shared, gripped mouth to mouth,
dozens mill about, hundreds.

Hundreds mill, thousands about—
space clears in the moiling crowd.

Gentle men pose with their catch.

Space cleared in the moiling crowd,
scent of gasoline, unwashed…

Unwashed scent of gasoline,
roiling tar, feathers flutter.

Roiling tar, fluttered feathers,
torch of twisted newspaper.

Cleared space in the moiling crowd.

Home is Where

Torch of twisted newspaper,
smoke from his own burning flesh.

From his own flesh burning, smoke.
Gelding, tongue swells, eyes boil, bulge.

Gelded, eyes swell, bulged tongue boils,
skin crisp as bacon, burnt toast.

Twisted torch of newspaper.

Flesh crisp as toast, burnt bacon,
mob'd dragged from a cabin bed.

Dragged from a cabin bed, mob-
stunned, tumbled-down, trodden, chained.

Down-trodden, tumbled—stunned—chained.
"Stick 'at boy lik' stickin' hogs,"

skin burnt crisp as bacon. Toast.

"Stick 'at boy lik' stickin' hogs
sizzled on a syc'more tree."

Sizzled on a syc'more tree,
flesh tore off piecemeal, scattered.

Flesh tore off, scattered piecemeal,
overalls baked, blood-dusted,

sizzled on a syc'more tree.

Caked, blood-dusted overalls
search ashes for souvenirs.
Ashes searched for souvenirs:
denim, fingerbones, tooth, ear.

Ear, teeth, fingers, denim, bones:
souvenirs. Postcards 10 cents.

Look pretty for the postcards.

Home is Where

A SINGLE MOTHER'S SONG

They cut me twelve inches,
right down the middle.
Twelve inches,
here.

Women are built to share.
Even our bodies are never our own.
But my body, was different,
only slightly,
but enough.
Enough for me to believe
that almost thirty years of erratic periods and medical complications meant
that I could take my body
and inhabit it
as my own.

My life was such that
I did what I wanted, when I wanted—
loved my family, loved my friends,
played godmother and adopted aunt,
spent or saved my salary as I chose.

My life was such that
I could move to any city,
for any period of time,
for any reason,
and leave
when I wanted.

My life was a Sex in the City dream.

At forty, I got pregnant.

To get pass the fibroids,
they cut me here.
When he came out,

he slept with his arms in the air,
still fighting against
the mounds of tissue
in my stomach
that made *him*
an impossibility.

It took thirty-eight days
for this open wound to heal,
layer by layer by layer.

His paternal grandmother believed herself
the matriarch of a dynasty,
to which I wanted to adhere myself through an heir.
She looked over her acres of giant watermelon,
towering corn, tobacco plants with leaves like blankets,
redwoods that led to heaven,
saw the power of her kingdom,
and thought I wanted to usurp her crown.
She didn't know my life
and he, the father,
wasn't one to oppose the queen.

I didn't mind that he wanted to test for paternity
because I knew *he* was already sure.
It was *she*,
the grandmother,
who wasn't.
I didn't mind when he wouldn't come to Lamaze classes
or doctor's appointments;
I didn't mind that he didn't offer to help financially
because my life was set.
I had biological family,
I had adopted family,
I had money.
What bothered me most was that,
even after the birth and test and apology,
he could still do whatever the fuck he wanted to.

No matter how much I talked,
I couldn't make him understand.

I had to move back home with my mom,
ten hours away,
to take care of her.
Cancer was new to both of us,
me and her.
Chemo.
Chemotherapy was the bull that was intended to repair the china shop.
I was tired.
She cared for me while I healed.
A few months later, I cared for her while she…

I couldn't work.
Twenty-four hours,
I was either nursing my baby
or my mother.
I was tired.

All this time, my baby has only seen his daddy four times,
but they talk on the phone.
Earlier today,
when they got off the phone,
he said to me,
"Mommy, my daddy's lost."
I said, "Baby, what do you mean?"
He just kept repeating,
"My daddy's lost. He can't find me."
Then he asks, "Can you find my daddy?"

When I got a moment to myself, I called him.
He said it would only be fair if I met him half way.
He said the word "fair."
To me. He said fair.
No matter how much I talked,
I couldn't make him understand
that I'm tired.

I'm exhausted.
I can't make that trip safely.
I can't leave my mom alone for that length of time.
But
my son specifically put me in charge of finding his daddy.
Just because I had an open wound, didn't mean he had to have one, too.
I got a cousin to look after my mom and I drove—
on Yellow Jackets and sunflower seeds,
with the windows down in forty degree weather
screaming to keep myself awake.

Even down to our bodies,
women are built to share.
We have to.
We can't just think of ourselves.
Just be to ourselves.
Just be ourselves.
But men...
This world was made for men to be selfish.

JUST BEFORE MIDNIGHT

One
The heart beat beating
Time beaten rock
Rocking
World weary
Rocking chair
Breathing breaths
Like ocean waves
Keeping time—
Borrowed—
By the yellow sun and red moon
Measuring time by storms
Rooting strong against
The wind
For the tiny,
Tiny
Syncopating
Hummingbird wings winging
Dropping drips
And swallowing spoonfuls
Of air
Unaware of suns and moons
And faces and hands
Just recognizing
That loving, gentle
Chilly touch
And the shared clockwork.

WHITE GIRL

They laugh.

White Girl

Tiny murders
from tiny dangers
fly
between the words.

White

beads click time
at the ends
of my plaits
between the claps
of rope on pavement.

White

ash smudges the webs
between my fingers
that the Vaseline missed.

Girl

unaware that colors
could act
and talk
I act
and talk

White

girls hold their forearms
over mine.
I hate how they spit

Home is Where

through tucked lips
and grinning teeth
Bl-a-cK.
The word cracks
like hot grease.
Not like home
where the word
rolls from the lips
to a soft stop
like chewing fresh rolls.

White

boy once sent me home
with the question,
that question,
"Daddy, what's a nigger?"

White

Girl

they call me.
Along their hairline
runs burns
from the hot comb
and no lye relaxer.

Another message comes
for the light-skinned girl
with the good hair.
"Twan say wha'sup."

Girl

unaware that colors
could act
and talk,

I act
and talk

White

Girl

They laugh.
Tiny red lines
show where tiny cuts
bleed on their lips.
Pieces of me
fall.
Chunks of my grandmothers'
"Be the smartest kid in your class."
Chunks of my grandfathers'
"Do your best, baby."
Chunks of my dad's
"Act like you been in public before."
Chunks of my mom's
"Behave like a young lady."
Fall
Cut to the ground by
"She think she too good"
by
"Oreo,"
by

"White

Girl"

aware that colors
could act
and talk,
I begin
to act
and talk

Black.

To Danya, My Daughter

After the choosing, earth
or a high crypt in the left arm
of the cross at Elmwood, after the strong arms
of your husband, your brother's tears, come tell
my spirit. After the long drive to leave me,
the slow black line, tell them the purple click
of my heels on the dance floor
and the swirls of silk
tickling my legs. Tell them the lines
I put down against
agony, the verse after verse
for joy. Tell them the times
I knew the Great Ancestor Goddess
would hold me above
that last shaking. Have them wear my shoes
and eat my lines. Then, come, daughter. Come
tell my spirit
again and again.
I will hear you
and I will
be glad.

"To Danya, My Daughter"
Dorothy Perry Thompson (1944-2002)
Copyright 1995

ABOUT THE CONTRIBUTORS

ANJAIL RASHIDA AHMAD, PhD. is currently the director of the Creative Writing program at North Carolina A&T State University. Ahmad won a Headlands Center for the Arts Residency and a NC Arts Council Artist Grant, she was also elected to the board of the NC ACLU. She received the Margaret Walker Alexander Award for Poetry, the Robert Frost Prize in Poetry, the Southern Literary Festival Prize for Poetry, and two Janef Preston Prizes for Poetry from the Academy of American Poets. Her poetry collections include, *the color of memory* (Clear Vision Press, 1997) and *necessary kindling* (LSU, 2001), a finalist for the Milt Kessler Book Award. Her poems have appeared in *The Black Scholar, Obsidian III, The African American Review, Washington Square Review*. She is founder of Black Ink Writers Workshop in Greensboro.

ACECILY ALEXANDER was born and raised in Charleston, SC. She is a graduate of the Charleston County School of the Arts. In 2006 she published, *The Crickets Know My Secret*.

MARCUS AMAKER was born in Las Vegas and lived in England, Texas, Japan, and Maryland before arriving on Charleston, SC in 2003. He recorded his first original music at the age of 8, and began writing poetry and working in graphic design in high school. He has published three poetry books, released seven self-produced studio albums and has been the catalyst for countless art projects, posters and websites. As a spoken word poet, Amaker has toured the country and performed for national television. Recently, Amaker launched a new publication in Charleston called *Charleston Scene*, through *The Post and Courier*, that focuses on art, music, theatre, poetry, movies and multi-media.

SHIRLETTE AMMONS is a poet, writer, musician and director of an arts program for children. Her collections of poetry are, *Matching Skin* (Carolina Wren Press, 2008) and *Stumphole Anthology of Backwoods Blood* (2002). She is also vocalist for hip hop rock band, Mosadi Music. Her poetry and essays appear in *The Ringing Ear: Black Poets Lean South, The Asheville Review, Obsidian* and other publications. She is also a Cave Canem Fellow, recipient of the Kathryn H. Wallace Award for Artists In Community Service and the United Arts Council Emerging Artist Grant for songwriting.

EARL BRAGGS was born in Hampstead, North Carolina, a small fishing community seventeen miles north of Wilmington. At present he is a UC Foundation and Battle Professor of English at the University of Tennessee at Chattanooga. His latest collection of poems, *Younger Than Neil* (2009) follows recently published *In Which Language Do I Keep Silent* (New and Selected) (Anhinga Press 2006), *Crossing Tecumseh Street, House On Fontanka, Walking Back From Woodstock* and the 1992 Anhinga Prizewinner, *Hat Dancer Blue*. He also published a chapbook of poetry titled Hats. His poems have appeared in *Ploughshares, Colorado Review, Crab Orchard Review, Connecticut Review, 100 Years of North Carolina Poetry*, and others. His novel in progress, *Looking for Jack Kerouac*, won the Jack Kerouac Prize in fiction and was a finalist in the James Jones First Novel Contest.

BUTLER E. BREWTON taught at Furman University for twelve years before taking an appointment as professor of English and Poet in Residence at the South Carolina State University. He is Professor Emeritus of Montclair State University in New Jersey after 25 years as a professor of English there before moving back to South Carolina, authoring and publishing *Richard Wright's Thematic Treatment of Women, Moon Pie*, an autobiography, *What Manner of Man* all in 2010. His collections of poetry are *Rafters and Other Poems, Indian Summer*, and *Stray Cat on a Dirt Road.*

LINDA BEATRICE BROWN (b. 1939) is a poet, novelist, and professor. She has one published volume of poetry, *A Love Song to Black Men* (1974), and her poetry has appeared in *Black Scholar, Encore, Ebony,* and *Writer's Choice*. In 1984 she published a novel, *Rainbow Roun Mah Shoulder* (under the name Linda Brown Bragg), and in 1994 an historical novel *Crossing the Jordan*. Her latest novel is *Black Angels*, published in 2009. She graduated from Bennett College in North Carolina, from Case Western Reserve University, and from Union Graduate School where she earned her Ph.D. Brown has taught at UNC-Greensboro, Guilford College, and Bennett College where she currently teaches.

CHRISTIAN CAMPBELL is the author of *Running the Dusk*, which was a finalist for the Cave Canem Prize and the Forward Poetry Prize for the Best First Book in the UK, and won the 2010 Aldeburgh First Collection Prize. A recent recipient of a Lannan Residency Fellowship, he teaches at the University of Toronto.

DAWNN CHANDLER is from Schenectady New York, where she attended the University at Albany, receiving a B.A. in English. In 1989 she moved to South Carolina where she has made her home ever since. Dawnn Chandler is a 2010 South Carolina Chapbook Contest winner for her book . Her work also appears in the anthology, *The Chemistry Of Color, Cave Canem South Poets Responding to Art.*

COLENA CORBETT's writings have appeared in *Obsidian, Folio, The Charlotte Observer,* and many other publications. She has studied at the Split Rock Arts Program, Hurston-Wright Foundation Writer's Week at American University, and many other artist programs for poetry. She is an M.F.A. student in creative writing at the University of South Carolina.

HOWARD L. CRAFT is a poet, playwright and arts educator. He is the author of a book of poems, *Across The Blue Chasm,* and the plays:*The House of George, The Wise Ones, Tunnels,The Vet Who Lived Underground: Dispatches from Beneath the Map, Caleb Calypso and the Midnight Marauders* and *The Super Spectacular Bad Ass Herald Jones.* He lives in Durham N.C.

JOANNA CROWELL, poet, playwright, actress, and director, holds a B.A. in Women's Studies and Social Justice and Peace Studies from the University of Western Ontario. She has been a member of numerous theatre companies, including The Actors' Theatre of South Carolina, The New American Stage Company and the African American Performance Troupe. In 1997 Crowell founded Ascension Theatre in Charleston, South Carolina, where she facilitates creative writing workshops for women and teens, and creates a platform upon which to perform their stories. She has performed her own poetry throughout the United States and Canada.

DéLANA R.A. DAMERON is the author of *How God Ends Us* (University of South Carolina Press, April 2009), chosen by Elizabeth Alexander as the winner of the 2008 South Carolina Poetry Book Prize. Dameron currently resides in Harlem.

MONIQUE DAVIS (Monique "1MOpoeticsoul"D.), is a native of Hartsville, South Carolina, a poet, spoken word artist, and activist for strengthening the arts and culture in our communities. She is a graduate of Colorado Technical University with a B.S. in Business Administration. Among the groups and organizations she is affiliated with are New Danger Poetry Group, S.T.R.U.G.LIN Life Changing Group, and Alternate ROOTs. She is also a Cave Canem South fellow.

Born in Ghana and raised in Jamaica, KWAME DAWES is the author of sixteen books of poetry and many books of fiction, non-fiction, criticism and drama. His poetry collection, *Hope's Hospice*, appeared in 2009. For many years he served as Distinguished Poet in Residence at the University of South Carolina. Dawes lives in Lincoln, Nebraska, where he edits Prairie Schooner and serves as the chancellor's professor of English at the University of Nebraska.

CELESTE DOAKS, poet and journalist, received the 2009 *Academy of American Poets* Graduate Prize and *AWP WC&C* Scholarship. Her journalism has appeared in multiple journals such as the *Village Voice* and *Time Out New York*; while her recent poetry can be seen in *Asheville Poetry Review, San Pedro River Review* and on*Torch.com*. Doaks is a member of CAAWC and received her M.F.A degree from North Carolina State University in May.

EBONIRAMM has partnered with both the SC Poetry Initiative and the Auntie Karen Foundation facilitating spoken word and poetry workshops in local schools. She has served as Poet–in-Residence of the Sumter Opera House in Sumter, SC and the Benjamin E. Mays Homestead in Greenwood, SC. Her career also includes a residency with VSA Arts of SC, in collaboration with United Cerebral Palsy of SC and GA and the Columbia Music Festival Association, as well as the release of her poetry CD "Passion" and her seminal jazz CD "The Look of Love." She is a Richland County Public Library (RCPL) Literary Resident and a featured musician of SCETV's education web portal www.knowitall.org.

PERCIVAL EVERETT is the author of three volumes of poetry, three collections of short fiction and seventeen novels. Among his books are *Erasure, I Am Not Sidney Poitier, Glyph, God's Country*, and *Frenzy*. He has been the recipient of the Pen-Josephine Miles Award, the Pen Center USA Award, the Academy Award from the American Academy of Arts and Letters, the John Dos Passos Award, the Believer Book Award, the Vallaombrosa Von Rezorri Prize and twice the Hurston/Wright Legacy Award. A recent inductee into the South Carolina Academy of Authors, Everett grew up in Columbia, South Carolina. He is the Distinguished Professor of English at the University of Southern California.

NIKKY FINNEY was born in Conway, South Carolina, in 1957. A professor of creative writing at the University of Kentucky and a Cave Canem faculty member, Finney is the author of four books of poetry including *On Wings Made of Gauze, The World Is Round*, and *Rice*, which won a 1999 PEN America Open Book Award. Her fourth collection of poems, *Head Off and Split*, was published by Northwestern University Press in 2011. She is also the author of *Heartwood*, a collection of short stories written especially for literacy students.

NICHOLE GAUSE resides in Charlotte, NC, with her husband and daughter. She was born and raised in Fort Mill, SC. Gause has won numerous awards including a North Carolina Artist Fellowship, a Semi-Finalist Award for the North Carolina State Story Contest, the Mecklenburg County Emerging Artist Award and a South Carolina Academy of Authors Poetry Fellowship.

JAKI SHELTON GREEN was selected as the first North Carolina Piedmont Poet Laureate in 2008 and received the North Carolina Award for Literature in 2003. She is the 2007 recipient of the Sam Ragan Award and a member of the prestigious North Caroliniana Society. Her poetry has appeared in publications such as Solo Press, The Crucible, The African-American Review, Obsidian, Ms. Magazine, Essence Magazine, KAKALAK, Emigration, Immigration, and Diversity, Callaloo, Black Poets Lean South, an anthology published by Cave Canem, the PEDESTAL Poetry Journal and Poets for Peace. Her publications include (Carolina Wren Press) Dead on Arrival, Dead on Arrival and New Poems, Masks, Conjure Blues, singing a tree into dance, breath of the song, and Blue Opal, a play.

TERRANCE HAYES was born in Columbia, South Carolina, in 1971. He received a B.A. from Coker College in Hartsville, South Carolina, and an M.F.A. from the University of Pittsburgh writing program. He is the author of *Lighthead* (Penguin, 2010), which won the National Book Award for Poetry; *Wind in a Box* (2006); *Hip Logic* (2002), which won the 2001 National Poetry Series and was a finalist for the Los Angeles Times Book Award; and *Muscular Music* (1999), winner of the Kate Tufts Discovery Award. He has been a recipient of many honors and awards, including a Whiting Writers Award, a Pushcart Prize, three Best American Poetry selections, and fellowships from the National Endowment for the Arts Fellowship and the Guggenheim Foundation. He is a professor of creative writing at Carnegie Mellon University and lives in Pittsburgh, Pennsylvania, with his family.

RAYCHELLE HEATH holds a B.A. in Languages from Winthrop University and an M.F.A in Poetry from the University of South Carolina. She has done numerous poetry readings, and served as an artist in residence for the Historic Columbia Foundation. She is currently teaching English in Majuro, Marshall Islands. Her chapbook *Between Tea Leaves and Tree Leaves* is available through *Thrift Press.* Her new book *Flying Away* is available on Lulu.com.

MONIFA LEMONS-JACKSON a.k.a. "Selah" was born and raised in New York City, where she attended the Black Spectrum Theatre Company and LaGuardia High School of Performing Arts. She was a founding member of Down South Syndicate, which created Columbia's first Slam Team. She is an Education major at Columbia College. She is a member of Cave Canem South.

A VAN JORDAN earned a B.A. in English literature from Wittenberg University in Springfield, Ohio, and an M.A. in communications from Howard University. He received an M.F.A. in creative writing from Warren Wilson College in 1998. Jordan's collections of poetry include *Rise* (2001), *M-A-C-N-O-L-I-A* (2005), and *Quantum Lyrics* (2007). *Rise* won a PEN/Oakland Josephine Miles Award and was selected for the Book of the Month Club of the Academy of American Poets. *M-A-C-N-O-L-I-A* received the Anisfield-Wolf Award. Jordan has been the recipient of a Whiting Writers Award and a Pushcart Prize. He has taught at a number of graduate writing programs, among them the University of Texas at Austin, Warren Wilson College, and the University of Michigan.

AJUBA JOY is a native New Yorker and long-time resident of Raleigh. She is a published poet, community advocate, activist, and leader. She is a graduate of Shaw University and NCCU where she earned a Masters in Public Administration. She has worked as a Health Educator at North Carolina State University. Ajuba Joy is the founder of ROOT1 (a community garden endeavor in Raleigh) and the owner of, Wellness Works Technologies and Joy Works Ink. She was awarded the Woman of Wake Award in 2009 by the Wake County Commission for Woman.

CATHERINE LAMKIN has been published in numerous anthologies. She hosted "Images in Flight" Literature Series in New York City featuring such writers as Terry McMillian and Wesley Brown. Catherine served as a contributing editor for *Central Park Journal on the Arts and Social Theory*. Catherine is also an artquilter. Her art quilts have been featured in museums throughout the United States. Her piece titled Change was part of an exhibit titled 44 Art Quilters for the 44th President and was exhibited at the Historical Society in

Washington DC. Catherine has been published in anthologies such as *New City Voices, Long Journey Home,* and *Central Park Journal on the Arts and Social Theory.*

KURTIS LAMKIN is a poet who plays the Kora. He has performed his work internationally at festivals, concert halls, prisons and universities. His poetry has been featured in *Paterson Literary Review, Crazy Horse, Black American Literature Forum,* and *Elements of Literature.* Mr. Lamkin was one of the featured poets on Bill Moyers' "Fooling With Words" television special. His animated poem "The Foxes Manifesto" was aired for two years on PBS. He has produced four cds that feature the kora and poetry: *El Shabazz, Queen of Carolina, Magic Yams* and an instrumental recording entitled *String Massage.* He is currently working on *Live Poem: a handbook for composition, performance and improvisation,* and a novel entitled *The Rest Of Us.* Kurtis Lamkin has taught with Teachers & Writers and the South Carolina Arts Commission; he has been Poet In Residence at The New School in New York and Georgia Tech.

GARY COPELAND LILLEY currently lives and teaches in Port Townsend, WA. He is a North Carolina native, a veteran of the US Navy Submarine Force, and a founding member of the Black Rooster Collective. He earned his M.F.A. at the Warren Wilson College Program for Writers. His awards include the Joan Beebe Fellowship and the DC Commission on the Arts Fellowship for Poetry. His publications include four books of poetry, of which the most recent is *Alpha Zulu* from Ausable Press..

At age nineteen, **ADAM DAVID MILLER** was jailed and exiled from Orangeburg, South Carolina for violating a racial taboo at 19 yrs. and has spent his adult life in California where he raised a family, prospered while working in education and supporting the arts.

INDIGO MOOR'S *Through the Stonecutter's Window* received the 2009 Northwestern University Cave Canem prize for a second book. His first book, *Tap-Root,* was published in 2006 by Main Street Rag. He is a Cave Canem fellow and a graduate member of the *Artist's Residency Institute* for Teaching Artists. Indigo is currently enrolled in the Stonecoast M.F.A. (University of Southern Maine) program where he is studying fiction, poetry, and scriptwriting.

LENARD D. MOORE, a North Carolina native, is Founder and Executive Director of Carolina African American Writers' Collective and Co-founder of Washington Street Writers Group. Moore's poems, essays and reviews have appeared in over 350 publications. His poetry appeared in over forty anthologies, including *The Bedford Introduction to Literature* (Bedford/St. Martin's, 2008), and *The Haiku Anthology* (Norton, 1999). His most recent book is *A Temple Looming* (WordTech Editions, 2008). He teaches at Mount Olive College.

PORCHIA MOORE is the former director of the Arizona Western College Creative Writing School, where she remains a professor of English at Arizona Western College. A graduate of the Citadel and The College of Charleston, her work has appeared in *Taboo, Red Lights, The George Street Observer, Miscellany, The Politics of Water, Drum Voices*, and several other publications. Her latest work is available in *Tempu Tupu/Waking Naked*, an anthology of Africana Women's Poetic Self-Portraits. She served as poet-in-residence at the Avery Research Center. Moore was also a judge at the 2006 Poetry Aloud finalist competition at the South Carolina Book Festival. She is currently building radio and community programs for the Yuma, Arizona, community and working on several collaborative projects.

MENDI + KEITH OBADIKE make music, art and literature. Their works include albums *The Sour Thunder* & *Crosstalk* (both on Bridge Records), a suite of new media artworks, *Big House / Disclosure*—a 200-hour public sound installation and book, the opera-masquerade *Four Electric Ghosts*, and a poetry collection—*Armor and Flesh*. Keith received a B.A. in Art from North Carolina Central University and an M.F.A. in Sound Design from Yale University. He is an assistant professor in the College of Arts and Communication at William Paterson University. Mendi received a B.A. in English from Spelman College and a Ph.D. in Literature from Duke University. She is an assistant professor of Media Studies at Pratt Institute and a poetry editor at *Fence Magazine*.

TANURE OJAIDE has won major national and international poetry awards, including the Commonwealth Poetry Prize for the Africa Region (1987), the BBC Arts and Africa Poetry Award (1988), twice the All-Africa Okigbo Prize for Poetry (1988 and 1997), and thrice the Association of Nigerian Authors' Poetry Prize (1988, 1994 and 2004). He has read from his poetry in different fora in Africa, Britain, Canada, Israel, Mexico, The Netherlands, and the United States. Some of his poems have been translated into Chinese, Dutch, Spanish and French. He is currently the Frank Porter Graham Professor of Africana Studies at the University of North Carolina at Charlotte.

GLENIS REDMOND is a native of Greenville, South Carolina. She graduated from Erskine College and received an M.F.A. in Poetry at Warren Wilson College. She is a Cave Canem Fellow and an NC Literary Fellowship Recipient from the North Carolina Arts Council. Her latest book of poetry is titled *Under the Sun.*

MICHELE REESE is an associate professor of English at the University of South Carolina Sumter where she also directs the South Carolina Center for Oral Narration. Her first collection of poems, *Following Phia*, was published by WordTech Editions in 2006. Her poems have appeared in several literary journals including Desire Street, *The Paris Review*, and *Valparaiso Poetry Review*. She lives in Sumter with her two sons.

JOYCE M. ROSE-HARRIS has been a resident of South Carolina since 1997. She was a fellow in the first class of Cave Canem South held in February 2010.

PHILLIP SHABAZZ is the author of two collections of poetry, *Freestyle* and *Visitation, and XYZoom*. His other book is a novel in verse titled *When the Grass Was Blue*. His poetry has appeared in *The American Voice, Obsidian II, The Louisville Review*, and on the North Carolina Arts Council's web site. Since 1994 he's been a visiting writer in many schools throughout North Carolina. He lives in Chapel Hill.

K.I.N.G. SHAKUR is a poet and community activist from Dallas, who has a passion for changing the world one word at a time. He is a graduate of Allen University in Columbia SC, and is perusing his MFA in poetry at Queens University in Charlotte, NC, were he resides. He is the president of New Danger Art collective, and has two published chapbooks.

EVIE SHOCKLEY is the author of *the new black* (Wesleyan, 2011) and *a half-red sea* (Carolina Wren Press, 2006). She is associate professor of English at Rutgers University, where she teaches African American literature and creative writing; she also co-edits the journal *jubilat*. Shockley lived for nine wonderful years in North Carolina (the Triangle and the Triad), during which she began seriously writing and publishing her poetry, and she still claims it as home.

SHARAN STRANGE grew up in Orangeburg, South Carolina. She is the author of Ash—selected by Sonia Sanchez for the Barnard Women Poets Prize—and other widely published poems and essays. Her honors also include awards and residencies from the Rona Jaffe Foundation, D.C. Commission on the Arts, Yaddo, and the MacDowell Colony. She is a contributing editor of Callaloo and board member of Poetry Atlanta. She teaches writing at Spelman College.

STEPHANIE T. SUELL retired from the U.S. Air Force, spends her days penning poetry and short stories. She is a self-published author of a poetry book, Reflections of Self, and a cookbook, Hot Water Cornbread. She resides in Columbia, South Carolina, and is currently working on a novel.

CEDRIC TILLMAN holds a B.A. in English from UNC Charlotte and graduated from American University's Creative Writing M.F.A. program. In March 2005, he was named a semifinalist in *The Nation* magazine's "Discovery" contest; in 2006, he was a finalist in N.C. State University's annual poetry contest. A Cave Canem fellow, Cedric's work has appeared in *Folio, Crosscut, Inspirit, The Drunken Boat* and *Kakalak 2009: An Anthology of Carolina Poets.*

CAROLYN BEARD WHITLOW is Dana Professor of English at Guilford College in Greensboro, NC, where she has taught since 1993. Finalist for the 1991 Barnard New Women Poets Prize, and the 2005 Ohio State University Poetry Prize, she published her first poetry collection, *Wild Meat,* in 1986 with Lost Roads and her most recent book, *Vanished,* won the 2006 Naomi Long Madgett Poetry Award.

CANDACE WILEY was born and raised on the border of North and South Carolina. She completed a B.A. at Bowie State University and her M.A. at Clemson. She is currently completing an M.F.A in fiction writing at The University of South Carolina.

PERMISSIONS

Hub City Press is an independent press in Spartanburg, South Carolina, that publishes well-crafted, high-quality works by new and established authors, with an emphasis on the Southern experience. We are committed to high-caliber novels, short stories, poetry, plays, memoir, and works emphasizing regional culture and history. We are particularly interested in books with a strong sense of place.

Hub City Press is an imprint of the non-profit Hub City Writers Project, founded in 1995 to foster a sense of community through the literary arts. Our metaphor of organization purposely looks backward to the nineteenth century when Spartanburg was known as the "hub city," a place where railroads converged and departed.

HUB CITY PRESS Poetry Titles

Waking – Ron Rash

Checking Out – Tim Peeler

Still Home: The Essential Poetry of Spartanburg – Rachel Harkai, editor

Hidden Voices – Kristofer Neely

Twenty – Kwame Dawes, editor

Noticing Eden – Marjory Heath Wentworth

Eureka Mill – Ron Rash